Praise for
Building the Enterprise of the Future

"This book provides a framework and the key ingredients needed to lead a successful enterprise in the age of knowledge."

Hassan Syed
Founder and CEO: Bir Ventures

"A holistic and insightful treatment of the key dynamics of the knowledge economy and enterprise - with an added bonus of 'How To' make it work for your organization. A must read for the 21st century organizational leader."

Dr. Michael Stankosky
Co-founder: Institute for Knowledge & Innovation;
Professorial Lecturer, Knowledge Management:
The George Washington University

"A clever book to tackle current uncertainties with certainty."

Dr. Charles Chow
Managing Director: East-West Group, Singapore

"Given the knowledge-based nature of today's work, and the collaboration complexities of today's organizations, this book provides the essential success principles for the future enterprise – which are actually needed today."

Dr. John Lewis
Author: The Explanation Age

"Anyone who wants to lead an Enterprise of the Future will transform the way they think about a firm's knowledge and its role in shaping the future of both business and society itself."

Dr. Dan Holtshouse, Director Corporate Strategy (Retired): Xerox

"I have read many multidisciplinary books. And yet, there was something different about this one. It raised two important questions: Where are we going, and why are we going there? After finishing the book one realizes that we need to be not only thinking about the future, but at the same time thinking about how to prepare ourselves to make that future better. Going through the book a second time not only helped clarify the questions, but deep personal answers began to emerge."

Dr. Kamen Lozev
Associate Professor and past Fulbright Scholar:
South-West University 'Neofit Rilski' – Blagoevgrad, Bulgaria

"From the midst of complexity, we've delved into the organization of the future and, somehow, when we think we're closer, there's always something new and different and wonderful to reach towards. This masterpiece becomes part of our ever-changing realities just ahead of time, that is, raising our awareness to future choices, the future that is already here and the one that is accelerating towards us. We are asked to embrace our role as co-creator and together, as eight billion interconnected minds, share and expand our knowledge to move into the future. This book serves to clearly and succinctly answer the question, 'How do we get there?'"

Dr. Alex Bennet, Mountain Quest Institute;
Professor of Knowledge and Innovation Management:
Bangkok University

"Dr. Art Murray's writings are akin to multiple courses of a 5-star internationally reputed restaurant: Each course (chapter) delights and enlightens; at the end you're booking a seat for the next gourmet offering!"

Dr. Francesco Calabrese
Founder/Executive Director: International Institute for Knowledge
& Innovation; Professor: Bangkok University

Building the Enterprise of the Future

Co-creating and delivering
extraordinary value in an
eight-billion-mind world

Arthur J. Murray

ISBN-10: 069294866X
ISBN-13: 978-0692948668

Published by: Applied Knowledge Sciences Press
Printed in the United States of America

Contents

BUILDING THE ENTERPRISE OF THE FUTURE

Manifesto

The world has become extremely complex and fast-changing.

This presents both challenges and opportunities.

Ignorance is the root cause of poverty and suffering.

Knowledge dispels ignorance.

By enabling knowledge to flow freely, people can make better choices and lead more enriched and fulfilled lives.

We need to bring this knowledge to bear if we are to overcome the challenges and seize the opportunities of the 21st century.

We are rapidly becoming a global knowledge economy of eight billion minds.

The social knowledge entrepreneur is a key player in the global knowledge economy.

Traditional business and organizational models impede the flow of knowledge and will not work.

The enterprise of the future must be able to innovate and learn at a rate equal to or greater than the speed of change in the market.

To achieve and sustain this level of performance, organizations must transform themselves from a knowledge-hoarding culture to one that freely discovers and shares knowledge.

This means changing the way we live, work and learn.

Those who refuse to change will be rendered irrelevant.

Original contributors: Alex Bennet, David Bennet, Francesco Calabrese, Kent Greenes, William Halal, Hugh McKellar, Mark Minevich, Art Murray, Joseph Okpaku, Sr., Michael Stankosky, Richard Van West-Charles.

BUILDING THE ENTERPRISE OF THE FUTURE

Forward

"Sustaining High Performance in a Flat World."

That was our initial goal back in February 2006, when over forty thought leaders, faculty, researchers, and practitioners in knowledge management and related fields gathered at The George Washington University Institute for Knowledge and Innovation. The occasion was the *First Executive Roundtable on the Enterprise of the Future.*

The discussion centered around three questions:

1. What's driving enterprise transformation, and what will happen if we don't adequately respond?

2. What will the enterprise of the future look like, and how will it be different from the enterprise of today?

3. How do we get there?

In the years which followed we've searched long and hard for the answers. Several of the graduate students, research faculty, and visiting fellows from industry and government who participated went on to complete their doctorates. In the process, they added to an ever-expanding body of scientific data and case studies, contributing valuable insights into how organizations can transform themselves in order to effectively compete in the 21st century.

Other members of our group went out into the trenches and applied the new ideas in practice, validating and refining what we discovered along the way. While "eating our own cooking," we began assembling a body of actionable knowledge regarding what works and what doesn't work in different types of situations. This included continually sharpening and refining the overall conceptual framework.

The thought processes and outputs of this amazing brain trust are provided in this book and associated website (enterpriseofthefuture.org). You, as an executive, manager, practitioner, or subject matter expert can use these resources to boost your professional and organizational performance in any number of ways. Over time, you'll begin to notice measurable improvements in learning rates, concept-to-development cycle times, and time-to-market (see Chapter 1: *Business at the speed of thought (almost)*).

Increased collaboration in global, virtual environments allows you to more quickly and effectively respond to and co-create new business opportunities. You become more competitive through lower labor costs and increased knowledge worker productivity. You gain increased return on your IT investment through more tightly aligned work processes, culture and enterprise architecture.

Growth in relative market value results from improved development, application, and expansion of key intellectual assets. Improved learning and better decision-making reduce risk, costs, and liability due to errors. Streamlined, rapidly self-organizing collaborative processes greatly increase your ability to quickly respond to, and even lead, major changes in your market.

Any one of these improvements alone will noticeably improve your top and/or bottom line performance. Two or more, and who knows how far you'll be able to go.

The changes you see in the market are irreversible. Those who recognize and capitalize on them will be rewarded. Those who don't will be rendered irrelevant.

The enterprise of the future is an ongoing quest. It's been said that we can either try to predict the future or we can co-create it. By building the capacity for rapid innovation and learning, the enterprise of the future serves as a model for sustained success in a complex, fast-changing world.

We hope you'll join us in leading, connecting, co-creating extraordinary value, and making breakthrough discoveries as we put our collective brain trust to work.

Preface

Perhaps you've noticed. Things are very different. And if on occasion they seem to be returning to normal, don't be fooled.

The changes we've seen in the early part of this century have forever transported us into a new world. It comes with a formidable set of challenges: globalization; increasing disintermediation and complexity; shrinking development cycles; loss of pricing power; massive shifts in consumer and workforce demographics; to name a few.

On top of it all, the speed of change is accelerating. This poses a threat to the very survival of many organizations as old, traditional business models fall by the wayside.

Until now, there has been little help available to respond to these challenges in a systematic way. Competing on a sustained basis in a global, knowledge-based economy demands wholesale changes in the way we live, work and learn. Even how we think, both as individuals and organizations, needs to change dramatically. This means envisioning and building the enterprise of the future.

We define the Enterprise of the Future as a self-organizing, adaptive, learning network of social knowledge entrepreneurs achieving mutual goals.

Such an enterprise must:

- Quickly learn and adapt to changes in the environment
- Find value where others can't
- Make enlightened business decisions
- Quickly and effectively carry out those decisions
- Measure outcomes and make adjustments
- Continuously innovate – driving changes in the market rather than vice versa.

Note that our definition stretches, even dissolves the boundaries typically associated with traditional organizations. From now on, when you think of enterprise, think *ecosystem*. And not just a biological or business ecosystem. Rather, a *total* ecosystem, encompassing business, society, the environment, and now, of course, increasingly "intelligent" machines.

Whether you are a leader, manager, or practitioner, the enterprise of the future framework provided in this book gives you the tools you need to compete in a complex, fast-changing global marketplace. It serves as a guide to formulating the right strategy, identifying and minimizing risk, and transforming traditional knowledge-hoarding organizations into agile knowledge enterprises.

The framework consists of four areas of transformation. These are derived from the widely adopted four pillars of knowledge management: *leadership, technology, organization, and learning*. These four pillars resulted from one of the first doctoral dissertations in the then-nascent discipline of knowledge management.[1] Since that initial work nearly two decades ago, the framework has undergone further validation and refinement in over two dozen additional dissertations, along with case studies and graduate student projects covering over a hundred organizations across a wide range of industries.[2,3]

Over the course of the past seventeen years, the original four-pillar framework has held firm, although different applications have resulted in slight changes to the nomenclature. For the purposes of building the enterprise of the future, we've adopted the labels of *leading, connecting, co-creating, and discovering*.

---

[1] Francesco A. Calabrese, *A suggested framework (4 pillars) of key elements defining effective enterprise KM programs*, D.Sc. dissertation, The George Washington University, Washington, DC, 2000.
[2] Michael Stankosky, ed., *Creating the Discipline of Knowledge Management*, Elsevier Butterworth-Heinemann, 2005.
[3] Annie Green, Michael Stankosky, and Linda Vandergriff, eds., *In Search of Knowledge Management: Pursuing Primary Principles*, Emerald Group Publishing Ltd, 2009.

Regardless of which terminology you choose, it all boils down to this…

If your speed of change – the rate at which your enterprise innovates and learns – is slower than that of your industry, you're continually falling behind in a vicious cycle.

Eventually you'll be out of business. If you want to succeed and grow, your enterprise needs to change at least as fast as, or faster than, the speed of change in your industry.

In the chapters which follow, we'll step through each of the four pillars of transformation, giving you specific ways to apply the key principles. But first, let's take a look at where we are today, how we got here, and some of the more interesting challenges and opportunities we will likely face in the months and years ahead.

BUILDING THE ENTERPRISE OF THE FUTURE

Part I

Raising the Bar

BUILDING THE ENTERPRISE OF THE FUTURE

Chapter 1

Business At the Speed of Thought (almost)[4]

Remember the *Beer Game*? In many ways, the Beer Game simulation is as popular today as when it was first introduced at MIT's Sloan School in the 1960's (different versions are still available through free software downloads). It's based on a scenario in which a beverage retailer, a distributor, and a brewery play supply chain tag while a steady, reliable product named Love's Beer experiences a spike in popularity resulting from an appearance in a hit music video.

From beginning to end, the entire simulation spans a period of about six months, which at the time of its release was considered to be a reasonable planning horizon. The object of the game is to maximize sales and profits, regardless of your position in the supply chain.

---

[4] Adapted from Art Murray, *Logistics at the speed of thought (almost)*, KMWorld Magazine, May, 2014.

Although there are a few break-even and winning strategies, most players end up flying their "opportunity" straight into the ground, as orders go unmet and inventory levels pile up just as the popularity of the runaway fad begins to wane.

If you're wearing your enterprise of the future goggles, you should begin seeing many of the intricate connections which make up the complex world of manufacturing and logistics. More importantly, you should be looking for ways to increase the speed by which a thought becomes an idea which leads to an innovation which becomes a product which, after working its way through a vast network of transportation, storage, distribution and delivery systems, ultimately results in sales.

As we move into the decade following the year 2000, the pace really begins to accelerate. In 2003 a beer game-like scenario was being played out across the ocean. Only it wasn't a simulation.

In November of that year, Spain's Crown Prince Felipe and a television newscaster named Letizia Ortiz announced their engagement. At the press event, which was televised to the world, the princess-to-be wore a white pants suit. Although rather uncharacteristic for old-world royalty, it generated a wave of excitement among young female viewers.

Seizing the opportunity, a Spanish fashion company named Zara quickly designed, manufactured, marketed, distributed and sold hundreds of look-alike Princess Letizia outfits. In later years, the princess herself could be seen occasionally sporting Zara apparel and accessories, helping to further boost the company's growing popularity.

The following year, as Madonna was launching her "Re-Invention" tour in Europe, one of Zara's designers took note of the megastar's blouse. Within three weeks, Zara had pushed a similar blouse out to its retail outlets. Hundreds were quickly sold, and fans could be seen wearing the blouse at the final concert of the month-long tour.

Now you might be thinking: producing and selling a few hundred pants suits and blouses at one time doesn't really amount to much. That's true, but only if your clock is running in the typical fashion industry cycle of spring, summer, autumn and winter. For Zara, their product cycle is as short as one week (the time it takes for them to cancel a product that isn't selling) to slightly less than a month. Zara replenishes its product line continually and opportunistically, rather than by a fixed, seasonal calendar. This results in customers visiting their 1,800 stores in major cities around the world three times more often than the industry average.

Discovering and connecting new dots

What do fish, fashion, and the Kalahari Desert have in common? Certainly not much. At least at first glance. But when you instill a passion for continued rapid innovation and learning, connecting such unlikely dots becomes commonplace.

It so happens that, in addition to fashion, the Spanish love to eat fish. They are second only to the Japanese in per capita fish consumption. And like the Japanese, slowing down the clock by selling frozen fish doesn't cut it. Their fish must be fresh.

The West African coast of Namibia is rich in the favorite and often rare varieties of fish the Spanish crave. But fishing is more an art than a science. And the catch of the day can vary widely, both in terms of variety and volume.

As described by MIT Professor Yossi Sheffi, the whole process, from net to table, usually takes from 24 to 48 hours.[5] As soon as the net is raised from the side of the fishing boat, it's emptied into the refrigerated cargo hold below.

As the boat heads for port, the skipper is already on a satellite phone, forwarding the details of the catch to Spain-based Caladero, a global fish processor and distributor. As soon as the boat skipper hangs up,

---

[5] Yossi Sheffi, *Logistics Clusters*, MIT Press, 2012, p. 1-17.

Caladero immediately begins soliciting advance orders from its vast network of food stores and retail outlets.

The boat arrives in port at Walvis Bay, Namibia. Since it's nearly 800 miles to the nearest suitable airport, the catch is quickly loaded onto refrigerated trucks with auxiliary fuel tanks needed to cross the scorching Kalahari Desert through Botswana and on to Johannesburg.

At the airport, the fish are loaded into a refrigerated warehouse, awaiting transfer to a Boeing 747 cargo plane. As you might expect, the process isn't always straightforward. Because the catch of the day varies in weight and volume, two critical variables in the world of freight, Caladero always keeps an eye open for other companies that might want to hitch a ride on the daily flight.

For example, Zara often has to quickly ship mohair and wool, both plentiful in South Africa, to respond to a celebrity "tweet," "like," or other instant trigger which puts the next rapid-turnaround fashion into motion. It's not co-incidental that both Caladero and Zara have major facilities at the 747's final destination: a massive logistics complex in Zaragoza, a city of about 800,000 inhabitants in the somewhat remote region of Aragón, Spain.

In a world in which manufacturing is outsourced to countries with the cheapest labor, Zara keeps its manufacturing operations local. To remain competitive the company relies on the rapid capture, transfer and application of knowledge. From knowing their customer and always staying one step ahead of emerging trends, to optimizing millions of lines of code that control robots, conveyors, sorting and packaging machinery, Zara moves one million items of clothing daily, drawing from an inventory of about 34 million. That's a monthly turnover of slightly less than 90 percent, an enviable metric in their industry.

Will Zara be able to sustain its agility as competitors respond with their own disruptive innovations? Or will Zara stay one step ahead by disrupting itself? Time will tell.

For now, Zara and Caladero together occupy a mere two percent of the 140 million square feet of space ultimately planned for the Zaragoza complex. Mentally extend that operation out to the remaining 137 million square feet, and you'll begin to appreciate the magnitude and scale of 21st-century logistics.

No matter what industry you're in, if you find yourself complaining about how long it takes to get something done, think about the amazing things happening in Zaragoza. If they can move fresh fish across thousands of miles of roads, desert, and ocean in less than 48 hours, there is no reason why your organization can't reduce your time-to-market cycle by fifty percent or more.

Chapter 2

Enterprise and Industry Clockspeed

In this chapter we define a key element that makes the Enterprise of the Future different from traditional organizations. While the contrasts are many, the main idea centers on the common themes of innovation and learning, the speed at which they occur, and their effectiveness.

A Simplified Enterprise Model

An initial step toward building an enterprise of the future is to express the main concepts and components diagrammatically as models, frameworks, and architectures. Let's start with a simple system flow diagram consisting of inputs, processes and outputs (see Figure 2-1).

At the center of any enterprise are people. People play a critical role at every point in the value network. Even at points where activity is fully automated, people are involved in the design of the automation system, monitoring its performance, stepping in when things go wrong, and thinking ahead to what the next generation of that system might look like.

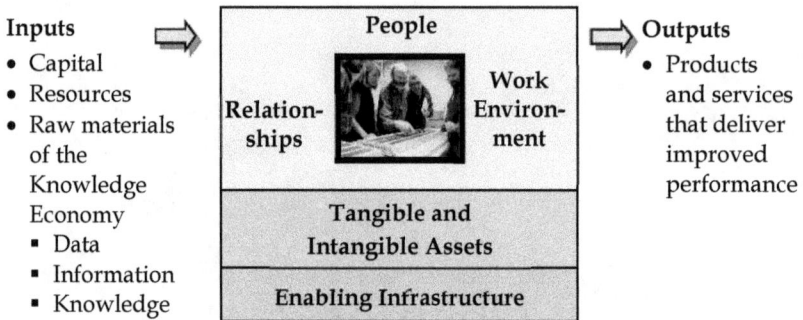

Figure 2-1. A basic enterprise system flow diagram

A large percentage of an enterprise's value lies hidden in the relationships which tie everyone together, including clients, suppliers, advisors, stakeholders, and many others. Finally, the environment you create for your people plays an important role in their performance.

The systems and processes for managing people, tasks and activities form the key assets of the knowledge enterprise. These assets fall into two categories: *tangible* and *intangible*. Tangible aspects are quite familiar: real estate, facilities, machinery, equipment, furniture and the like. Intangible assets, which can account for more than eighty percent of your organization's total value, need far greater attention than they traditionally receive.

Aside from a devastating fire or similar catastrophe, you usually don't have to worry about your final assembly building being carted off by a thief in the night. But your intangible assets are another matter.

Whether it be the sudden departure of a key employee or a cyber-attack resulting in the compromise of your most valuable trade secrets, these are often the most vulnerable and pose the greatest risk. While tangible asset management has been around for a long time, we are still trying to wrap our arms around the intangible, often not even knowing exactly what those assets are or what to call them.

Holding everything together is the enterprise's infrastructure, represented by the bottom block in Figure 2-1. Without an enabling infrastructure, the best-designed enterprise is lumbering and inefficient.

Taking a look at the various inputs, the traditional ingredients have been and still continue to be financial capital, natural resources such as air, water and fuel, and other raw materials feeding the production, packaging and delivery of finished goods. However, attention must now be given to the intangible raw materials of the knowledge economy: data, information and knowledge.

Like any system, when inputs are fed through and processed by the various elements of the enterprise, output products and services are produced, delivered and supported. Sustained success is determined by the value the market believes it is receiving for the enterprise's output. For a consumer it could mean a more comfortable lifestyle, or better health and well-being, all of which come from increased knowledge. For an enterprise, the perceived value is likely to focus on improvements in top and bottom line performance, improved chances for mission success, market growth, and the like.

Let's examine how these elements combine to perform the two most critical activities of an enterprise of the future: *innovation* and *learning*.

Innovation

While much of the attention in building knowledge enterprises is focused on learning, such as *the learning organization*, we've recently seen increased emphasis on innovation. Both are equally important. Learning can be viewed as looking in the rear-view mirror and adjusting accordingly. Innovation can be thought of as turning off the GPS and plowing new ground. Even exploring uncharted territory.

One of the reasons innovation often takes a back seat to learning is that learning usually occurs as the result of the successes and failures of others. In other words, someone else has already taken the risk. Innovation requires embracing risk and accepting failure, albeit in a managed (as opposed to chaotic) way. The estimation that over 95 percent of attempted innovations fail doesn't help matters, especially in cultures prone to punish, rather than learn from, failure.

Back when things moved more slowly, many organizations applied the successful strategy of sitting back and watching others take the arrows. They would identify which innovations were gaining traction. They would then adopt those innovations while riding the uptrend. But as we've seen in Chapter 1, the game of playing catch-up is growing ever more difficult.

So what's an organization to do? It may sound mundane, but the first step is to change the mindset of your workforce regarding innovation. One way to do this is to provide a safe proving ground where new ideas can be developed and tested. The promising ideas can continue to advance in stages, while failures are treated as learning experiences which benefit the entire enterprise.

Learning

Learning is meaningless unless the lessons being learned are correctly *applied*. It's a continuous process, but it can be extremely difficult to implement in practice.

For example, during an economic downturn, fear often takes over. Training budgets are among the first items to get slashed. This slows down the speed of innovation and learning. Mistakes are repeated, making things even worse.

Organizational learning is not rocket science. In its most basic form, it consists of asking a few very simple questions...

What was done, when, and by whom? What was the result? What worked and why? What didn't work and why not? How will you do it differently next time?

Repeat.

Clockspeed

Understanding clockspeed is the key to designing and implementing the right innovation and learning systems for your enterprise.

The notion of clockspeed was introduced into the mainstream in the late 1990s by MIT Sloan School professor Charles Fine.[6] Fine's work covers several types of clockspeed. These include product clockspeed, process clockspeed, and organization clockspeed.

Product clockspeed refers to the time between successive generations of a product family. This is a crucial aspect in many industries, especially consumer electronics, medical devices, and clothing.

Process clockspeed can vary significantly, ranging from periods of relative stability on one hand, to wild price and volume variations on the other. Organizations that do not continuously review and update their processes – at least at the same rate as the changes driving the value of their products and services – will suffer steady erosion of both profits and market share.

Organizational clockspeed covers everything from changes in the C-suite to ownership changes to complete business model re-design. For organizations closely linked to government, changes in heads of state, legislative bodies, or the judiciary can have equally significant impact.

For our purposes, *industry clockspeed* is the aggregate speed of change in your industry or market segment. It takes into account all three areas of product, process, and organization. On one end of the spectrum you have the decades-long clockspeed of highway construction and jet

---

[6] Charles H. Fine, *Clockspeed: Winning Industry Control in the Age of Temporary Advantage*, Basic Books, 1998.

aircraft. On the other end, entertainment and consumer electronics.

While industry clockspeed focuses primarily on external factors, *enterprise clockspeed* represents the speed at which an enterprise innovates and learns. Both notions are illustrated by the four clock icons in Figure 2-2.

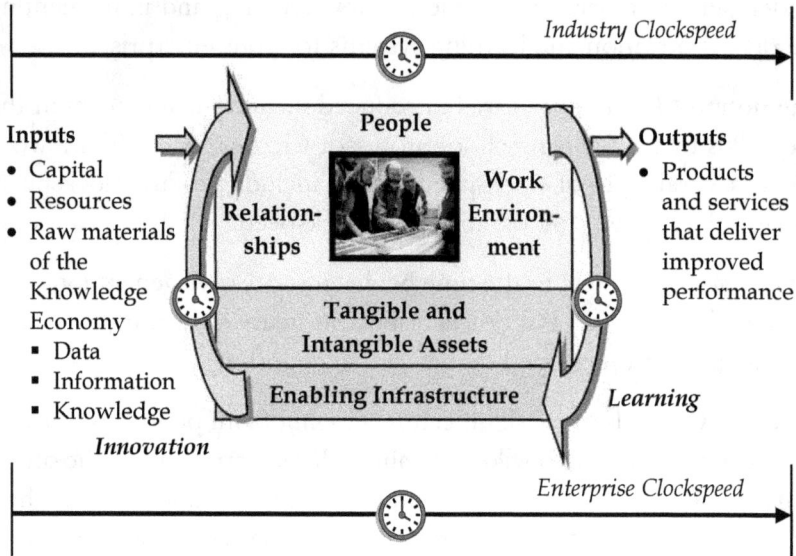

Figure 2-2. Comparing enterprise and industry clockspeed

Although these will vary somewhat, some key elements which drive enterprise clockspeed include:

- Product development cycle times
- Design pipeline
- Employee engagement and turnover
- Learning rate (including ability to scale)
- External workforce characteristics such as:
  o Unemployment rate
  o Number of skilled workers.

You now have a key metric you can use as a guide in building and sustaining a knowledge enterprise. Just be sure to keep in mind the following:

T*he speed at which your enterprise learns and innovates must be equal to or greater than the speed of change in the market.*

A note of caution: because of the complexity of the many variables involved, Fine strongly advises against placing too much effort in coming up with hard numbers or metrics relating to clockspeed. Rather, it is more important to view clockspeed on a relative basis. In other words, it's more important to know if you are keeping pace or falling behind, rather than attempting to measure the precise rate of change.

With an improved understanding of clockspeed as a backdrop, we've set the stage for building a framework by which you can identify and manage the key elements which drive the speed of innovation and learning within your enterprise. But first, let's take a look at how we got to where we are today.

Part II

How We Got Here

Chapter 3

A (Very) Brief Economic History of the World[7]

For much of recorded history, when tribes and nations weren't waging war and raking in spoils, economic activity consisted mostly of the exchange of tangible goods and payment for the labor to produce those goods. Those goods were, and still are, perishable and non-perishable.

For example, avocados are perishable, having an extremely brief shelf life. Avocado farmers have a very narrow time window in which to harvest their crop. They have an even narrower window in which to sell, regardless of economic conditions.

---

[7] Adapted from Arthur J. Murray and Matthew E. Sekella, *Building the enterprise of the future: How the new knowledge economy is changing the ground rules*, VINE: The Journal of Information and Knowledge Management Systems, Volume 37, Number 2, 2007, p. 91-99.

Oil, on the other hand, has an extremely long shelf life. It doesn't need to be harvested at any particular time. If market demand is soft, it can remain in the ground indefinitely until prices reach more profitable levels. Leakage of inventory is virtually non-existent. Since land doesn't depreciate, property taxes are often the only major expense.

When competition is fair, price is determined by supply and demand. If supply outstrips demand, the price decreases accordingly. Declines of fifty percent or more are not uncommon. If the price gets high enough, extraction methods which were previously deemed too costly, such as extracting oil from coal or shale, begin to emerge, ultimately re-exerting downward pressure on prices.

The underlying force in determining demand is perceived, or subjective, *value*. Even for something in very short supply, if its perceived value is low, it will command a low price. This holds true for oil, avocados, and especially *information*.

Information used to be like oil. It took a long time to produce, was available in limited quantity, and had a relatively long shelf life. The invention of the printing press greatly improved the production and availability of information, and its contribution to economic growth eventually became more significant.

The second half of the twentieth century changed everything. The invention of the transistor, and later, the integrated circuit, ushered in a wave of technology that greatly accelerated the production and dissemination of information. Information became like avocados. Its value (price) rapidly diminishes over time, as illustrated in Figure 3-1.

What determines the value of information, that is, the price the market is willing to pay? You've probably heard the term "information overload." Clearly, the supply of information has greatly expanded, aided by technologies that render it cheap and easy to produce in virtually unlimited quantity. Yet some information providers such as International Data Group (IDG) are consistently growing their revenues and profits. Their ability to generate economic wealth on a regular basis demonstrates that it's possible to achieve and sustain profitability in an information-saturated world.

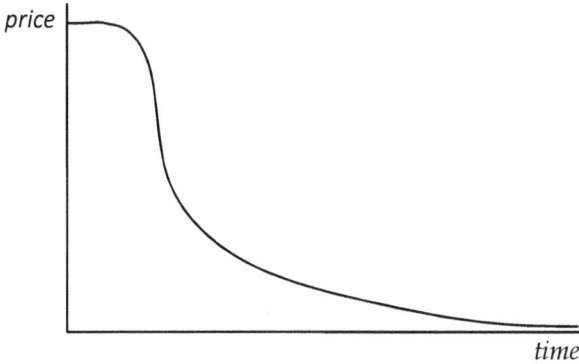

Figure 3-1. The value of information rapidly diminishes over time

The evolution of information as an economic good

Information has always played a crucial role in the global economy. Throughout history, spies provided valuable intelligence regarding an adversary. One example is how the fate of the newly independent United States of America rested on the skills, complex relationships, and dangers faced by George Washington's key espionage agents.[8]

In the 16th century Sir Thomas Gresham used privileged information to make extraordinary sums by engaging in one of the earliest versions of currency arbitrage. The result was *Gresham's Law* which is still widely quoted in economic circles today.[9]

---

[8] Alexander Rose, *Washington's Spies: The Story of America's First Spy Ring*, Bantam, 2006.
[9] Gresham, a member of the Court of King Henry VIII, knew that the monarchy planned to systematically debase the coin of the realm by mixing gold with other, less noble metals. Understanding that "bad money chases good money away" (Gresham's Law), he used this information to sell British Sovereigns short, while going long in Dutch Guilders, thereby becoming one of the world's first successful currency arbitrageurs. A fascinating account of his life can be found in Perry Epler Gresham and Carol Jose's book: *The Sign of the Golden Grasshopper: A Biography of Sir Thomas Gresham*, Jameson Books, 1995.

From Gresham's time up until a few decades ago, financial information was extremely costly to produce and obtain. As such, it was available almost exclusively to large institutional investors and a select few high-net-worth individuals. With the advent of the internet this type of information became more ubiquitous. As the supply steadily increased, its value began to drop.

In today's markets, information needs to be acted upon quickly. The greater the number of traders that have access to information, the faster the information degrades in value. Millions of investors now engage in online trading, and the bulk of the information they obtain is free. Assuming the absence of a monopoly, the low cost is a reflection of its true market value.

Another example of the drop in the value of information can be seen in the widespread popularity of the online encyclopedia *Wikipedia*. Traditional encyclopedias such as *Encyclopædia Britannica* were at one time elegant appointments in many homes, and were excellent sources for a wide variety of information. Many sales professionals began their careers selling encyclopedias from door-to-door, making handsome commissions in the process.

Why did something that was so valuable become essentially free virtually overnight? For one, vastly improved means of production and distribution obviated the need for many elements in the encyclopedia supply chain. The public had the knowledge, and through the technology of the wiki was willing to freely share that knowledge. On the supply side, editorial boards, sales departments, and printing presses were no longer necessary, driving down the costs of production even further. In addition, there was no longer any reason for consumers to have to wait an entire year to receive an update, as online encyclopedias now provide those updates instantaneously and automatically.

Another distinguishing characteristic of encyclopedic information is that it consists primarily of factoids. In today's fast-moving world, the value of facts and figures has dropped appreciably. This is due in part because on the demand side, consumers derive very little benefit from having large collections of facts and figures on their bookshelves.

Instead, the greatest value comes from information that's *predictive* and *actionable* in nature. Such information allows buyers to anticipate what's going to happen so they can take economic advantage of events as they unfold.

For example, realtors no longer have a monopoly on housing market data. Home buyers empowered with information that was previously unavailable to the general public can now quickly access home prices and appraisal values, school district ratings, tax and population trends, all online and for the most part, free of charge.

Even when it comes to obtaining financing, home buyers no longer have to sit behind an imposing mortgage lender's desk. Instead, they freely search online to find the most favorable terms.

The upshot is that people now have instant access to a wide variety of previously unavailable information. This includes information regarding health issues, treatment options, and potential side effects of prescription drugs. Car, home, and business owners no longer need to go through an agent, along with the associated price markups, in order to obtain insurance. Only those agents who have been able to deliver extraordinary value have remained in business.

Which brings us to the question: if information is becoming commoditized, is in oversupply, and continues to have an increasingly shorter shelf life, what's an information provider to do? The answer is: *become a knowledge enterprise.*

Enter the Knowledge Economy

Like its industrial-age predecessor, a knowledge enterprise takes the raw materials of data and information as inputs. Through the application of innovative processes, it then generates new, high-value, actionable information, i.e., *knowledge.*

Knowledge has value for many different reasons, depending upon the targeted application. It can help users identify which data are most relevant to their situation. It can help them analyze that data in the right way and help determine the best course of action to take.

Knowledge can also perform, in varying degrees, in the presence of incomplete or incorrect information. Most importantly, knowledge helps people make better *decisions*. The greater the impact of those decisions, the greater the value of the knowledge being produced and delivered.

Let's return to the example of the avocado farmer. Climate, weather, crop varieties, nutrients, soil conditions, land topography, costs and availability of labor (which in many parts of the United States, for example, consists primarily of foreign itinerant workers), and many other factors determine the quality and yield of the crop being produced. Predictive information regarding each of these factors can be generated by analyzing and extrapolating a variety of raw data from public and private sources.

Applying knowledge gained through learning, experience, and trial and error to the analysis results, along with a dose of innovation, greatly improves the chances for success. Success may include a variety of factors such as profitability, humane working conditions, sound business ethics, environmental quality, as well as avoiding fines, asset forfeitures, and even jail sentences for regulatory violations. For our avocado example, when all of these elements come together in an efficient and effective way through a tightly integrated *knowledge enterprise*, the outputs benefit not only the farmers, but also the workers, suppliers, distributors and consumers – everyone in the value network.

People will gladly pay a premium for this new type of manufactured good, i.e., knowledge, to the extent that the premium offsets risk and maximizes reward. This is the essence of the new knowledge economy. However, we still need to address one major element: the *perishability* factor.

"Business at the speed of thought"[10]

Given the relentless persistence of price degradation of information, the only way to retain value in a fast-changing market is through consistent rapid innovation and learning. Rapid innovation means *quickly discovering and creating new value in response to or in anticipation of changes in technology, market perceptions, and the like.* Rapid learning means *observing and evaluating not only those changes, but also the effects of an innovation once it has been introduced.*

The value of the resulting knowledge can follow two paths. When left on the shelf, like avocados, it will quickly depreciate. Unlike avocados however, the more knowledge is consumed, the more valuable it can become. That's because the production, distribution and consumption of knowledge are part of a continuous cycle of innovation and obsolescence. Figure 3-2 illustrates this notion.

Returning to the example of the avocado farmer, let's say Knowledge Enterprise #1 develops an algorithm that results in a five percent increase in crop yield. This helps determine the algorithm's value. But a five percent increase may not be enough in absolute dollars to be of interest to a small avocado farmer. However, some of the larger farms might be willing to pay a substantial premium as long as the algorithm continues to produce consistent results.

Let's say the larger farms buy or license the algorithm. Knowledge Enterprise #1 now enjoys the financial rewards of its innovation.

Knowledge Enterprise #2 gets wind of this and comes up with a new innovation that improves the yield by up to eight percent, a three percent increase. Overnight, the value of Knowledge Enterprise #1's innovation has dropped. This follows the pattern in Figure 3-2.

---

[10] The title of a book by Bill Gates, Warner Books, 1999.

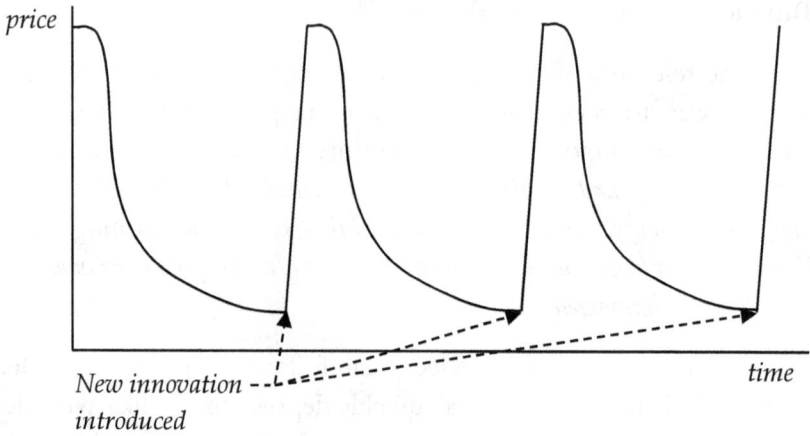

Figure 3-2. The perishability of information demands frequent innovation to maintain profitability

This need not be the end for Knowledge Enterprise #1. The drop in the value of their algorithm now makes it affordable to smaller farmers, resulting in additional revenue at a small incremental cost.

Let's say a third knowledge enterprise which serves the hedge fund industry has expertise on reducing risk. It uses innovation to produce a variant of their financial risk-reduction algorithm. When applied to avocado farming it does not necessarily increase yield, but substantially reduces risk.

Avocado farmers, large and small, now have even more knowledge available for purchase. But because of resource constraints, they may be faced with choosing one approach over the other, potentially limiting the market share of all three niche providers. In the meantime, Knowledge Enterprise #4, a decision support software vendor, sees this as an opportunity and produces a software application to help avocado farmers balance yield versus risk.

Now consider the addition of easy-to-write, inexpensive mobile apps which produce "mashups" of satellite imagery and other data such as weather patterns, soil moisture, etc. You can see a virtual cottage industry in the making here.

Once the "seed" of innovation is planted, knowledge can quickly grow, moving across industry sectors. And the wealth produced can continue to grow indefinitely as long as the innovation process is sustained. The term "indefinitely" is appropriate because no raw materials are extracted or consumed other than the brainpower employed by the various knowledge enterprises, which is theoretically unlimited.

This raises an interesting question: what happens when billions of individual knowledge entrepreneurs come online? Like Wikipedia, as soon as something is posted it's viewed, analyzed, validated, and/or revised almost instantaneously.

Each individual mind is potentially a knowledge micro-enterprise. The expected result of such massive disintermediation is the continued compression of the development cycle, which demands progressively faster innovation. This continually accelerating process of innovation is illustrated in Figure 3-3.

What does an eight-billion mind economy look like?

The ability to quickly build and grow a knowledge enterprise is a serious game-changer. You don't need to own any land. Just a brain and a computer with internet access will suffice.

Take a look at Table 3-1. If you own or have stake in an oil field or avocado farm, you are one of about 65,000 or 100,000 respectively, in the global marketplace. Care to guess how many potential competitors you have as a knowledge worker? Try 3.7 billion and growing. And that doesn't even begin to take into account the AI-based systems that are steadily appearing online and gaining increased autonomy and decision-making capacity.

price

New innovation --
introduced

time

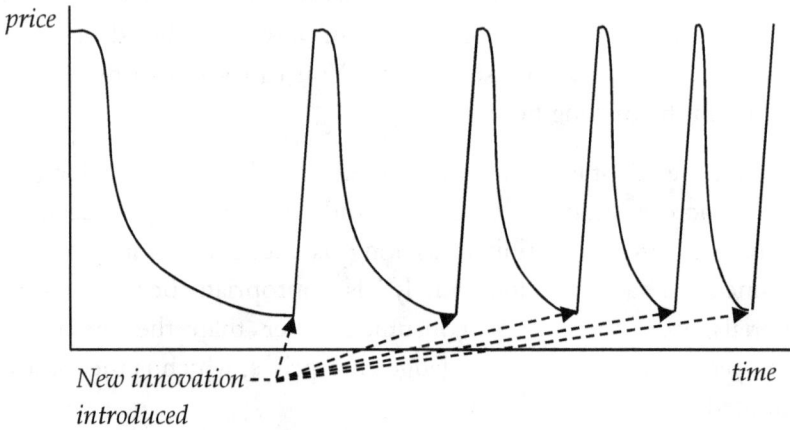

Figure 3-3. Progressively shorter product life cycles require more frequent and rapid innovation

Table 3-1. The knowledge economy is approaching and even exceeding "business at the speed of thought"

Product	Approximate number of competitors worldwide	Average product shelf life
Oil	65,000 oil fields	Æons
Avocados	100,000 farms	1-4 weeks
Knowledge	Over 3,700,000,000 minds connected to the internet	Varies widely, but can be milliseconds, as in the case of high-frequency securities trading or cyber attacks

The knowledge economy opens up the possibility for a totally new paradigm in which billions of minds are brought together as collaborators, stakeholders, regulators, competitors and consumers. Just as the industrial age gave rise to the middle class, the proliferation of knowledge micro-enterprises creates the potential for an unprecedented expansion of wealth, especially near the bottom of the pyramid.

We're not just talking about financial wealth. Such massive interconnection builds a structural foundation for enhancing and enriching all aspects of life by enabling the cross-fertilization of innovations among many different industries. But it's the speed at which all of this takes place that will determine the difference between success and failure.

We'll take a look at speed. But first we need to understand the means by which value is measured and exchanged in a speed-of-thought economy.

Chapter 4

Money 3.0[11]

You want to develop a new product or service. Expand your market. Attract, hire and retain the best knowledge workers. But there's one nagging issue that keeps coming up. It goes by different names: working capital; budget; financing; funding. Or just plain *money*.

As of this writing, there are a handful of large companies that can be referred to as cash rich. According to Moody's Investors Service, five companies (Apple (AAPL), Microsoft (MSFT), Alphabet (GOOGL), Cisco Systems (CSCO) and Oracle (ORCL)) are sitting on half a trillion dollars of cash or cash equivalents. That amounts to nearly one third of the $1.7 trillion in cash and cash equivalents held by all non-financial companies in the US at the end of 2015.[12]

---

[11] Adapted from Art Murray, *The Future of Money*, KMWorld Magazine, January, 2017.

[12] usatoday.com/story/money/markets/2016/05/20/third-cash-owned-5-us-companies/84640704/

The stark reality, however, is that many small-to-medium-sized companies and organizations are cash poor. If you're in the first category, great. Being an enterprise of the future will help you stay there. If not, you can still make it, but you'll have to do things a little differently.

Most people tend to look at money simply in terms of dollars and cents. Or in denominations of one of the other four globally traded reserve currencies.[13]

Clearly, it's much more complicated. And like many aspects of today's global marketplace, it keeps changing at an ever faster pace. So before we get into preparing for what lies ahead, a brief history is in order...

Money 1.0

Things were simple back in the good old days. You could take a one-ounce silver coin and cut it into eight equal slices, just like a miniature pie. These were called "pieces of eight." Two bits were a quarter, or 25 cents.

As people got tired of lugging around chests full of precious metals, paper currencies began to pop up. These included "certificates" redeemable into very precisely weighted pure metal ingots.

Under this system, the value of a dollar remained reasonably stable. That is, until August 15, 1971, when President Richard Nixon declared that the United States would no longer convert dollars to gold at a fixed rate. Which brought us to...

Money 2.0

All those redeemable certificates were eventually replaced by notes backed by the "full faith and credit" of the issuer. Freed from the

---

[13] In addition to the US dollar, the International Monetary Fund has designated the Euro, British pound, Japanese yen, and Chinese yuan as the world's basket of reserve currencies.

redeemability requirement, the supply of US notes in circulation skyrocketed. Since Nixon's 1971 pronouncement, the money supply as measured by the U.S. Federal Reserve's M2 indicator increased nineteen-fold from $686 billion to $13.6 trillion.

During that same period, debt in all US economic sectors went from $1.7 trillion to $63.5 trillion, a 3,800% increase. Anxious to get in on the game, many other countries followed suit.

And just like those annoying gold bars, why have all that paper sitting around? After all, we're in the digital age! Paper money, bonds with coupons, and stock certificates have mostly been replaced with zeroes and ones. The movement of money is now limited only by the speed of light and the bandwidth and storage capacity of the servers and networks connecting them.

But why stop there? Derivatives, complex financial instruments representing "bets" on the future value of underlying digital assets, have exploded to the point where nobody knows how many have actually been issued. Estimates of the value of all derivatives worldwide run as high as $600 trillion. Compare that to a global GDP of around $74 trillion, and you quickly realize that such leverage is unsustainable over the long run.

And just in case you think we're being excessively US-centric, 60% of the entire global economy is dollar-based, and 88% of all foreign exchange trading involves the US dollar, with daily volume in the $4-6 trillion range.[14]

The upshot of all of this is frightening. We're talking about over half a quadrillion dollars in the form of binary electronic signals stored in servers all across the globe. Which brings us to...

---

[14] More detailed data, scholarly papers and other information are available at the Federal Reserve's economic research website at fred.stlouisfed.org.

Money 3.0

Cryptocurrencies are an attempt at reining in the runaway freight train by imposing limits on the amount of money that can be created out of thin air. But like their traditional cousins, cryptocurrencies are denoted by a single trading unit such as a bitcoin.

In response to this limitation, multi-faceted forms of value exchange based on integral accounting are beginning to emerge. One of the leading examples was developed by Dr. David Martin. In addition to money, Martin's framework consists of five other key forms of value exchange: *commodity; custom & culture; knowledge; technology; well-being.*[15]

Dig deeply enough, and you'll find no shortage of instances in which each of these six forms of value exchange are being applied. For example, many investment funds are devoting significant percentages of their portfolios to *impact investing*. For these funds and like-minded organizations, performance is measured using the *triple bottom line* of *financial-social-environmental* return.

The knowledge component is particularly interesting. Many designers now share their intellectual property with manufacturers and vice versa. Sometimes billion-dollar companies merge without a single unit of currency changing hands.

What it all means

Whether one or more of these alternative forms of currency become mainstream remains to be seen. But you can count on at least two eventual outcomes.

First, the current credit-driven system will come to an end, either gradually or cataclysmically. It simply is not sustainable. Second, one or more new forms of currency will take its place, possibly a hybrid which combines financial, social, and other measures.

---

[15] globalinnovationcommons.org/integral-accounting

In less than half a century, money has moved from being a simple, reliable, commodity-based medium of exchange to a massive, complex web of mostly credit-based transactions. This precarious setup can change you and your organization for better or worse, literally overnight.

One thing to remember is that no matter what form it takes – metal, paper, or electrical impulses – money is simply a means for measuring, storing, and exchanging value. Nothing more, nothing less.

As such it will always be subject to attempts at distortion, manipulation, seizure, and theft. This introduces an element of uncertainty which can have serious consequences for those who don't adequately anticipate and prepare for the inevitable changes.

This is where agility comes into play. There is no way you can accurately predict what will happen and when. But big changes in the global monetary system are coming. Agile, knowledge-based enterprises will have the best chance of making it through these changes.

We will always need some form of money. The good news is that in a global knowledge economy, other modalities of value exchange are also possible. Trading arts and culture for food, energy and water. Or technology for health and well-being. The possibilities are endless.

Start putting your brain trust to work figuring out how best to make use of these different forms of currency. Or perhaps even discover some new ones. By doing so, you might just end up with a generous portion of the good old-fashioned variety jingling in your pocket as well.

Part III

The Case for Change

There's one thing you can count on. Sooner or later, whatever you're reading about in this book will change.

Although by no means complete, the next two chapters highlight eight challenges and eight opportunities that will likely have a major impact on the economy, business, technology, the environment, and society as a whole.

Challenges can be turned into opportunities, and vice versa. For purposes of discussion, each disruption has been placed into the category where the impact will likely be the greatest.

For example, cybersecurity is an obvious challenge when it comes to reducing vulnerability to attack or compromise. But it also presents a business opportunity in terms of prevention and detection.

The same goes for nanotechnology, which can be used as both a weapon, and as a beneficial delivery mechanism, such as for targeted medicine. Autonomous robots and drones can deliver pizza, or deadly chemical/biological agents.

The enterprise of the future aims to quickly respond to these challenges and opportunities by: 1) discovering and applying breakthrough innovations; 2) learning from the experience; 3) making adjustments.

Take heart. As the size of our massively-interconnected global mastermind reaches into the billions, you'll be more than up to the task...

Chapter 5

Challenges

We could devote an entire book to the serious challenges we will likely face in the coming decades. These challenges spring from many different sectors: finance; environment; health; education; energy; religion; culture; defense; security. You name it.

At the same time, a challenge in one sector affects other sectors to varying degrees, including society as a whole. For example, technology-driven threats have an adverse effect on business, the economy, and society. This in turn impedes innovation and slows down the evolution of technology, which further reduces innovation and economic development, continuing in a vicious cycle.

Table 5-1 lists eight of the more notable problem areas you should have on your radar screen. These are not listed in any particular order. It would be futile to do so, especially given how rapidly things change and priorities shift.

Table 5-1. Eight potentially destructive trends (challenge disruptors)

1. Increasing speed and complexity (the "five V's")
2. Technology-driven social amplification/attenuation
3. Complex, asymmetrical warfare
4. Natural and man-made disasters
5. Public health issues and concerns
6. Infrastructure vulnerabilities and needs
7. Outdated/unsustainable socio-economic models
8. Long-term consequences of business and political decisions.

Looking over the list, you might wonder: why all the emphasis on destruction? The answer is: it's just the nature of the world in which we live (bear with us, we'll get to the positive aspects of disruption in Chapter 6).

Most of the challenges we face are borne out of imbalances fueled by stress, conflicts, disagreements and other negative influences. As much as we like to emphasize the positive, we ignore the destructive forces in the world at our peril. They're simply not going to go away.

The best we can hope for is to put into place systems and processes to prepare for, detect, prevent, and respond to threats in ways that result in the least damage while consuming the least amount of resources.

Challenge Disruptor #1: Increasing speed and complexity (the "five V's")

Every day the world seems to "kick it up a notch," especially in terms of speed and complexity. One way to characterize these changes, at least with regard to the flow of information, is to use what are commonly referred to as *"the five V's:"* volume; velocity; variety; veracity; value.

Volume is the amount of information that needs to be managed. *Velocity* is the speed at which that information must be acquired and processed. Information covers an almost infinite *variety* of topics, sources, formats and applications. And it must be timely, valid, and reliable (*veracity*). Of course, none of this matters if the information does not provide *value* to a decision maker, whether human or machine.

The increase in the five V's continues to accelerate. As a result, decision makers can become easily overwhelmed to the point that the pressure to make decisions before assimilating and considering critical information can result in unacceptable risk or loss. This drives the need for faster, better, and more consistent decision-making through automation. This is where AI will play an ever-increasing role in the coming years.

However, the growth in the volume of data has and will continue to outpace our ability to assimilate and process it. The amount of data generated per day doubles approximately every nine months.

There are many contributing factors. One of the more important is data analytics, also referred to as "big data."

The emergence of big data analytics is a natural outgrowth of the ongoing increases in computation and storage capacity. As such, it relies mostly on brute force processing capability, with some algorithmic efficiency thrown in for good measure.

Analytics faces the challenge of keeping pace with the growth in data volume, now running at roughly five petabytes per day – 90 percent of which is unstructured. The types of data continue to grow as well, spanning biometrics, financial transactions, social and news media, email, and the IoT, slowly stretching the boundaries toward what might be called the *analytics of everything*.

When it comes to data analytics, it should become obvious that eventually we're going to reach our limits. Data are nothing more than measurements of observable epiphenomena (what we see on the surface level). These measurements are often inaccurate, incomplete, and lacking sufficient context.

To make matters worse, most of our predictive models attempt to take past history and extrapolate forward through various statistical methods including regression, cycles, etc. Occasionally inference techniques such as induction give us insights into what's going on underneath. We call these hidden layers *deep structure* (see Opportunity #7 in the next chapter). Even so, the picture which emerges is often incomplete. As a result, despite all our computational and algorithmic capacity, we still manage to get caught by surprise.

A good example is the actuarial sector. Insurance companies can tell you within a percentage point or two the probability of an adverse event, such as a loan default, occurring. There are even re-insurance companies which insure the insurers!

This all works fine, until the bigger picture changes, as was the case in the financial crisis of 2008. Financial markets run well when everything remains within historical boundaries. But the global economy is really a combination of artificial and natural systems, including social systems with dominant psychological and emotional components. Herein lies the shortfall with predictive systems based on data alone.

There are many different approaches to data analytics. *Cognitive computing* (moving human cognitive capability into the machine space) will play a key role in this evolutionary process.

Just as in the case of artificial intelligence, there is no universally agreed upon definition of cognitive computing. One of the industry leaders in the field, IBM, defines cognitive computing as "*systems that learn at scale, reason with purpose, and interact with humans naturally.*"[16] Rather than being explicitly programmed, these systems learn and reason from their interactions with users and from their experiences with their environment.

Other approaches apply complex statistics and inference algorithms, aided by raw computational power. However, the massive increases in

---

[16] Dr. John E. Kelly III, *Computing, cognition and the future of knowing: How humans and machines are forging a new age of understanding,* IBM white paper, October 2015.

data volume have begun to expose two shortfalls in these approaches: 1) little or no consistency in how hypotheses are generated and tested; 2) critical connections and gaps are often overlooked because of increasing data complexity and a growing number of interdependent variables. In addition, because predictive analytics are based solely on the past and use historical data to extrapolate into the future, these methods are especially weak in their lack of ability to confidently predict emerging socio-economic and political trends and events.

Another major shortfall is that current methods tend to limit the analysis to a single domain. This is becoming more problematic as today's complex world increasingly involves interaction across multiple interdependent domains. Such linkages are extremely difficult to identify using traditional data extrapolation. Relying on traditional methods of data analysis creates increased exposure to "black swan" events, and produces predictive behaviors that can actually make us more vulnerable to threats and other disruptions.

Challenge Disruptor #2: Technology-driven social amplification/attenuation

You've probably seen more than a few chaotic scenes unfold right before your eyes. You might view them either up close in person, or from a safe distance on a screen.

If you're like many, you might have asked, "How could this happen so quickly?" The reality is that in today's massively networked world of instantaneous communication, a tiny spark can quickly unravel into a major event. That's what we mean by technology-driven social amplification. It can also work in the opposite way. An event can be portrayed in such a way that the populace ignores it out of fear of reprisal.

Authors Nick Pidgeon, Roger E. Kasperson and Paul Slovic have discovered how hazards, both actual and perceived, can interact with psychological, social, institutional and cultural processes.[17] As you might expect, the ultimate outcomes tend to be highly unpredictable. They run the gamut from panic-induced boycotts to shutting down supply lines to rioting in the streets. Any one of these or similar situations can make it extremely unsafe for people to go to work or to the store to buy food, medicine and other basic necessities.

This is a risk you can't ignore. Over two-thirds of the U.S. adult population get their news from social media. This means that public opinion can change at light-speed as a single phrase or "meme" becomes wildly exaggerated.

Online radicalization also contributes to socio-political upheaval. It's further compounded by greater numbers of people entering what's referred to as the *dark web*. This is a collection of websites that use anonymity tools to hide their IP addresses.

The explosion in online activity has also resulted in the steady erosion of privacy. And lack of privacy doesn't apply solely to online communication. Recent events, including the 2016 US presidential election, have shown that even private telephone conversations are fair game for being reported on the evening news.

In short, because of this amplification/attenuation effect, you can expect competitors as well as hostile state and non-state actors to continue to seek and exploit weaknesses not only in your network and infrastructure, but in your people and processes as well.

Challenge Disruptor #3: Complex, asymmetrical warfare

Despite tremendous growth in human achievement and knowledge, many choose to avoid the study of warfare on the grounds that it's just plain "uncivilized." Unfortunately, warfare has always been a part of human history. And there is nothing to suggest that this won't be the case in the foreseeable future. To ignore this and not make plans to

---

[17] Nick Pidgeon, Roger E. Kasperson and Paul Slovic, *The Social Amplification of Risk*, Cambridge University Press, 2003.

prevent and mitigate damage is both reckless and irresponsible.

We've recently witnessed some interesting developments not only in conventional weapons (things that go "bang") but also in the silent realm of cyberwarfare. Here things don't go "bang," they simply go *dark*. The *WannaCry* ransomware attacks, which disabled systems including hospitals, railroads and other critical functions in over 150 countries, is a prime example.

In either case, the potential exists for the emergence of new weapons of previously inconceivable horror. Some examples include:
- Nano-weapons (including nanorobots, swarm intelligence)
- Untraceable toxic agents
- Extension of the battle theater into space
- Potential disruption of communications, power grids, food and water supplies, and the crippling of emergency care.

Any of the above threats alone has the potential for plunging the world into economic recession/depression. Ethnic and religious conflict, terrorism, and war can result in massive population migration, and even genocide.

This raises some key questions. Why do groups want to wreak such havoc and destruction, regardless of the costs? How can warfare be prevented, and if it cannot, how can the long-term effects of super-weapons be prevented or minimized? A major challenge for the coming decade is building resilience into our increasingly complex and vulnerable world of massively interconnected and interdependent systems.

Challenge Disruptor #4: Natural and manmade disasters

Natural and manmade disasters of recent years have made their impact felt in various ways, including protracted, costly recovery periods. While we've been very fortunate to date, relatively speaking, we can't help but wonder what would happen if the stresses on the system were to ratchet up several more notches. A bio-terror attack, for example, could cause serious supply chain, utility, emergency and other essential service disruptions lasting for months, rather than days or weeks.

Being able to recover from such an event would require heretofore uncharted degrees of resilience on the part of companies, organizations, agencies, municipalities, states, nations, regions, and the world as a whole. If you think that's trying to take on too much, recall that we have already experienced situations in which the actions of just one or two individual companies have had global economic repercussions.[18] Like it or not, the price we pay for a massively interconnected world is that small perturbations can be either quickly absorbed or just as quickly avalanche into a catastrophic system failure.

Challenge Disruptor #5: Public health issues and concerns

Public health concerns cover a wide range, from bio-terrorism and pandemics to caring for a growing and aging population. As medical knowledge grows more complex, so do the chances for errors. For example, despite the two trillion dollars spent on health care in the U.S. each year, over 1.5 million people are adversely affected by medical errors, including 100,000 deaths.[19] This is more than the number of people that would perish if one Boeing 737 jetliner crashed each and every day.

If a jetliner crashes, the response is always quick and decisive. A massive investigation is undertaken. Other flights involving similar aircraft are often grounded. Clearly, our demands for safety in air transportation far exceed our demands for medical safety.

It's not that new medical knowledge isn't being generated. Rather, dissemination and application are unacceptably slow. According to the

---

[18] At $600B, the Lehman Brothers collapse in 2008 remains the largest bankruptcy in US history; the ensuing collapse in the securities markets erased nearly $10 trillion in market capitalization.

[19] Institute of Medicine, Board of Health Care Services, *Preventing Medication Errors: Comprehensive Strategies for Reducing Drug-Related Mistakes*, National Academies Press, 2006.

U.S. Department of Health and Human Services, it takes 17 years, on average, for medical evidence to work its way into practice.[20]

Yet despite the long vetting process, the chances of misapplication are high, along with the associated costs. For example, the costs for corrective treatment for the 1.5 million people adversely affected by medical errors runs approximately $3.5 billion a year.[21]

The 20th-century approach to pharmaceutical development, production and distribution is not only unsustainable, but also reductionist approaches have resulted in increased toxicity and long-term adverse side-effects. A longer-living population requires new approaches to health and wellness.

Basic human needs such as food and clean water are also likely to command increased attention in the coming years. For example, efforts to achieve maximum levels of production have severely stressed the earth's biological ecosystem. Topsoil levels that have been maintained for centuries are dangerously low. To make matters worse, a disproportionate amount of agricultural resources are used for animal production and more recently, biofuels. In the meantime, human malnutrition and starvation continue on a large scale.

This issue is closely related to public health and wellness. In our current mass-produced system of food preparation and distribution, only a very small percentage of the nutrients present at the source ever make it into the human physiology.

Direct correlation between human intelligence and nutrition has also been proven. A prosperous global knowledge economy requires a well-nourished human population. New, sustainable approaches to food production need to be developed that can provide adequate nutrition for a growing and aging society.

---

[20] U.S. Department of Health and Human Services, *Summary of Nationwide Health Information Network (NHIN) Request for Information Responses,* June 2005.
[21] Institute of Medicine, Board of Health Care Services, *op cit.*

Challenge Disruptor #6: Infrastructure vulnerabilities and needs

There is hardly a place on earth that isn't in need of infrastructure attention. This includes the need for new infrastructure in emerging economies as well as the repair and upgrading of aging infrastructure in developed countries.

The infrastructure supporting the movement of people and goods all over the world is more than a century old and in various stages of deterioration. According to a widely-read study by the American Society of Civil Engineers, fourteen infrastructure areas in the U.S. including aviation, drinking water, roads and bridges rate a "C" or "D" with an estimated cost to repair of $1.5 trillion.[22]

Now would be a good time to re-evaluate our mass market, mass production mentality. It might not be feasible to spend trillions repairing and maintaining an infrastructure system that was built on the premises of the last century: plentiful fuel, clean air, and a supply chain based on the easy and rapid shipment of goods anywhere on the globe.

Likewise, we do not want our actions to have unintended consequences. Take, for example, the shortages in some poor areas that have resulted from the diversion of food crops to biofuels. Rather, we need to approach such problems systemically and look for solutions that are both structurally and environmentally sound, with the capacity to support sustained economic growth. It's time to consider new models that seek to maximize the transfer of knowledge, as opposed to finished goods, in order to enable a more robust capability to meet consumer demand. Or better yet, to meet basic human needs.

Critical resources such as food, clean water, timber, fossil fuels, rare earths, minerals, and metals, all need supporting infrastructure. In many ways we need to completely rethink how we generate, transport, use and recover our resources. Drone delivery systems, the "make"

---

[22] American Society of Civil Engineers, *Infrastructure Report Card*, 2005.

economy, and localized energy sources such as solar, wind, geothermal, and thorium (see Opportunity #1 in the next chapter) are just a few of the many trends you need to be tracking.

Challenge Disruptor #7: Outdated/unsustainable socio-economic models

Politically sensitive issues often end up as the elephant in the room nobody wants to talk about. Take, for example, the ongoing shift in demographics resulting in fewer workers paying into a welfare system supporting a growing population of retirees. Combined with unprecedented deficit spending, taxation, monetary expansion, and instantaneous global currency and derivatives trading, you have all the elements for a perfect economic storm.

The inevitable and painful downward adjustments will likely come at a time when increased investment is needed to reduce our vulnerability to the various threats we've mentioned, any one of which could bring the whole house of cards crashing down.

Bloated, centralized governments, whose budget growth consistently exceeds GDP growth, are unsustainable. In the last few decades, large corporations with literally dozens of layers of middle management were forced to downsize. Governments and government-sponsored organizations will now be forced to do the same. For example, since 1989, the U.S. Air Force has absorbed manpower reductions of 40%, with continued reductions expected for the foreseeable future.[23] Yet the service must still meet its present and future missions in the face of a rapidly changing threat.

---

[23] Lt. Gen. Roger Brady briefing, *Building the 21st Century Air Force*, June 2006.

And what of commerce itself? Even if we're fortunate enough to avoid widespread collapse, the forces of change continue to exert their influence. Governments and constituents alike are discovering that we are reaching the upper limits of the amount of money that can be taxed, borrowed, printed and spent.

How long our traditional systems of banking, taxation, regulation and commerce will hold up in a speed-of-thought world is an interesting question. The time has come to rethink how we measure, exchange, and grow value publicly and privately in a knowledge-based economy. Just a few of the many challenges include:

- Economic disequilibrium (over-expansion/collapse)
- Debt/equity leveraging/de-leveraging
- Excessive student debt; low return on education investment
- Inability to adequately enforce ever-expanding government policy, taxation and regulation
- Restrictive trade policies and imbalances
- Intellectual property theft/piracy
- Shifting demographics and preferences (workforce, consumer, etc.)
- Legacy institution dissolution.

Challenge Disruptor #8: Long-term consequences of business and political decisions

At no other point in history has mankind had the power to manipulate both living and inanimate matter at its most fundamental level. The long-term implications of genetically-engineered plant and animal species (not through traditional cross-breeding techniques, but through artificial manipulation and creation of genetic material) are unknown. Once destructive strains enter the gene pool, it's almost impossible to eradicate them. Many decisions made by scientists today will have lasting implications, good and bad, for future civilizations.

We need a more robust means of guiding critical decision-making in order to minimize the potential for long-term catastrophic consequences that are possible from the manipulation of the fundamental building blocks of nature. This means developing comprehensive bio-ethics codes and corresponding cultural transformation strategies.

Call to action

As significant as these eight challenges are, we've barely scratched the surface. At the very least, they should serve as a clarion call to raise our awareness about the serious dangers we're facing. Even normal, everyday changes require a never before seen degree of foresight and agility. Add the risks of high impact, low probability events, and the need for the fast-learning, adaptive enterprise has never been greater.

There are many other risks you need to be mindful of. Most are interconnected and interdependent. One can easily lead to another and then another in cascading fashion.

Perhaps most important of all is the risk of disruptive innovation. In the next chapter we'll take a look at how you can turn these risks and challenges into opportunities, if you play your cards right.

Chapter 6

Opportunities

Every major challenge presents unlimited opportunities for innovation. One advantage we still have is that Moore's Law never fails to disappoint. The introduction of new technologies and the steady performance gains of existing ones continues unabated. From cloud computing to mobile applications to exploding bandwidth, the capacity for connecting, co-creating and discovering through a global network of billions of minds is staggering.

An enterprise of the future must take full advantage of these trends. While by no means complete, Table 6-1 summarizes eight of the more noteworthy developments to which you need to be paying close attention. Just as with the eight challenges we discussed in the previous chapter, these eight opportunities will have a major impact on almost every industry sector, and society as a whole.

Table 6-1. Eight potentially beneficial trends (opportunity disruptors)

1. New, localized, sustainable energy sources
2. Continued exponential growth of digital processing, storage and bandwidth
3. Reduced trust footprint technologies and practices
4. The new AI: "Just-ahead-of-time" (anticipatory) systems
5. Human-technology integration
6. Integrative medicine and increased longevity
7. Connection to deep structure
8. Eight billion minds and 100 billion devices.

Opportunity Disruptor #1: New, localized, sustainable energy sources

As our knowledge-based world continues to evolve, you can expect that the insatiable need for energy will continue to grow along with it. For example, the US Intelligence Community's massive data center at Camp Williams, Utah is believed to require 65 megawatts of continuous electricity along with up to 1.7 million gallons of water every day for cooling. Yet this represents only a fraction of the power demand for the ever-expanding processing, storage, and transmission capacity springing up in cloud-based server farms all over the world.

Energy makes up about 7% of the world's economy. Without energy, everything we've discussed and will discuss in the remaining chapters would be meaningless.

Within the next two decades, we'll need energy for another 2 billion people. And that's only with regard to new capacity. We're not even talking about what we'll need in order to maintain and replace our aging and rapidly deteriorating infrastructure.

Of course we also know that the flow of energy must be clean, safe, abundant, and reliable. The problem is, we can't possibly build enough wind turbines, solar collectors and geothermal plants to even make a dent in the demand. Besides, if you remove many of the subsidies and other artificial advantages most renewable energy producers enjoy, they quickly become as much as 3-4 times more costly on average than legacy sources such as coal and nuclear.

But wasn't harnessing nuclear energy our ticket to unlimited supplies of electricity? At least that was the vision at the end of World War II. Instead we now have countries abandoning nuclear power altogether. In addition, large tracts of uninhabitable land in places like Fukushima and Chernobyl have sprung up, along with more than 52,000 tons of radioactive waste currently being stored in the United States alone.

You might be surprised to learn that we could be much further along in our quest for clean, plentiful energy were it not for a small body of critical knowledge that was lost over half a century ago.

Back then Alvin Weinberg, a Ph.D. mathematical biophysicist and administrator of the Oak Ridge National Laboratory, was looking for a way to use nuclear energy to power aircraft engines. Using liquid fluoride thorium, the experiment quickly evolved into the development of the molten salt reactor. A great example of connecting, co-creating and discovering!

As a nuclear fuel source, thorium has an impressive array of benefits. It's widely abundant. China, for example, has an estimated 20,000-year supply. It's extremely stable. Its radioactive waste remains toxic for a relatively short few hundred years. Best of all, thorium-based nuclear energy can be produced locally with relatively low capital investment.

Compare these benefits with the more than 400 uranium-based power plants currently in operation around the globe. Uranium and its waste products are extremely hazardous. They can quickly become unstable, require tightly controlled containment environments, and their toxicity lasts hundreds of thousands of years. Uranium-based power generation also requires significant capital investment (tens of billions of dollars per plant).

Alternatively, estimated costs for liquid fluoride thorium reactors run approximately 40% cheaper than coal and 80% cheaper than wind or solar energy.[24] Unfortunately for a variety of reasons, both political and nontrivial engineering challenges associated with commercializing the concept, the program has gone nowhere since it was shelved many decades ago. Now China, with the backing of several private venture partners, is picking up where Oak Ridge left off, and is pushing development of the liquid fluoride thorium reactor forward.

We're not necessarily advocating one form of energy over another. That's not our purpose. Nonetheless, we all have a role to play, to varying degrees, in making sound choices. Choices not only with regard to energy, but water, food, and other life-sustaining resources as well.

Opportunity Disruptor #2: Continued exponential growth of digital processing, storage and bandwidth

It seems like every time we think we've finally reached the limits of a particular technology, a new breakthrough comes along, smashing the supposed barrier. Moore's Law, that technology performance (typically referring to processing speed) doubles every 18-24 months, is the gift that keeps on giving.

It wasn't that long ago when many believed that we had finally reached the limits of microprocessor performance. After all, the 0's and 1's could only propagate through the silicon circuits no faster than the speed of light. Even with sub-micron-sized transistors, this limitation of physics would finally place a ceiling on the growth in performance we've been enjoying for decades.

Then along comes quantum computing. Still in the experimental stage, quantum computing uses multiple-state quantum bits (qubits) to perform large numbers of calculations on a single processor. This

---

[24] Robert Hargraves, *Thorium: energy cheaper than coal*, 2012.

creates the potential for solving what traditionally have been intractable problems such as decrypting encoded messages, or solving multi-body problems in physics.

To date, only a very limited number of quantum computing operations have been physically demonstrated in the laboratory. However, this technology is rapidly gaining adoption in the form of simulations on digital supercomputers.

Like many emerging technologies, the real breakthroughs ultimately occur when two or more are blended together in synergistic ways. Some promising technologies that may combine well with quantum computing are:

- Nanotechnology
- DNA computing
- Homorphic processing
- Electronic quantum holography
- Photonic computing
- Quantum cognition and quantum machine learning.

We won't go into each of these here, but it wouldn't hurt to do some exploration on your own. You'll likely find many of these technologies to be quite fascinating, even possible candidates for further development within your own organization.

Also on the horizon is a processing architecture that uses the propagation of holes as opposed to electrons. Curiously, this is being referred to as positronic processing, possibly bringing us closer to the positronic brain depicted by the character *Data* on the television series *Star Trek: The Next Generation.*

In summary, quantum computing is a development trajectory that bears close watching. One thing to look for is quantum computing resources that will eventually make their way into the cloud, bringing them more within reach of the small-to-medium enterprise.

Opportunity Disruptor #3: Reduced trust footprint technologies and practices

To succeed in a world filled with deceit, you need high levels of trustworthiness. That means considering human nature as well as technology. To better understand this, we've come up with something called the *trust footprint*:

Trust footprint = (custodians + systems) x (volume of information)

In the above expression, *custodians* represents the human element, which is built primarily on culture. For example, travelers in some parts of the world marvel at how shop owners leave their doors unlocked when they go for a break or to a nearby room for prayer.

In other parts of the world, you'll find the same types of stores with an array of security cameras, thick metal doors and multiple locks. That's the *systems* or technology component attempting to compensate for bad human behavior.

Volume represents the explosive growth in the number of information workers, along with the millions of lines of code and petabytes of data with which they are entrusted. All of which present far too many opportunities for unscrupulous individuals to hide in the shadows.

It essentially boils down to this: the greater the dependency on the human component, the greater the risk of a breach of trust. This is a natural consequence as an organization expands. The risk is compounded as the expanding organization naturally starts breaking up into smaller, increasingly isolated units.

The same goes for systems. The greater the volume and complexity, the greater the security risk from "back doors" and the like.

So where's the opportunity? Innovations that reduce trust vulnerability in one or more of these areas will have huge payoff potential.

Opportunity Disruptor #4: The new AI: "Just-ahead-of-time" (anticipatory) systems

Before we discuss the future of AI, let's first address the so-called "singularity" which seems to be on everyone's mind. Borrowed from the campy 1984 sci-fi flick *The Terminator*, "singularity" is the term given to that rapidly approaching point at which machine processing and memory capacity exceed that of the human brain.

We see evidence of this happening already, as AI-based systems are starting to outperform humans in certain areas. Examples include medical diagnosis, securities trading, facial recognition, including lip reading, and of course, a variety of games.

The fear among many is that if we don't act now, intelligent, autonomous machines will eventually take control over everything we do. Or according to a more benign scenario, machines will eventually do everything while we humans slowly turn into vegetables.

In such a world, machine intelligence becomes deeply embedded in every electronic device, including automobiles, mobile devices, heart pacemakers, appliances, the power grid; the entire IoT universe. Many believe that at some point these intelligent devices will begin to self-organize and assume control. The fact that such a possibility is extremely unlikely will have little bearing if an uninformed public believes that it's real.

The reality is that the singularity will likely be a snoozer, just like the dreaded Y2K event. And like Y2K, the singularity should be viewed as a technology milestone. Nothing more, nothing less.

As for fears about the onset of a *Skynet*-like apocalypse in which a single entity, human or artificial, controls everything, remember this simple law: *the more complex a system becomes, the more energy it consumes.* Eventually it collapses under its own weight.

There will always be limits. You can always count on the "*S*" curve. So stop worrying. Instead, you should be asking: *how can we make best use of the relentless increase in processing, storage and bandwidth capacity to take our systems to the next level?*

The number and complexity of the various pieces to be integrated keeps expanding. The field of AI alone encompasses many disciplines: cognitive science; human and machine learning; decision and game theory; knowledge engineering and management; natural language text and speech understanding and generation; philosophy (including epistemology, logic, and reasoning); robotics; machine vision.

In the closely-related field of data analytics, a more knowledge-based approach which uses anticipatory models is needed. This new, model-based approach will be less susceptible to the inherent flaws in reductionism and determinism, which generate fragmented results that come from holding most variables constant or ignoring them altogether. Natural, biological ecosystems, including social systems, do not always operate so deterministically. Instead, they are anticipatory in nature.

Robert Rosen was a pioneering researcher in this area and developed many of the initial theories of anticipatory systems.[25] Some basic behavioral characteristics include: understanding that behaviors can be both associative and non-associative; that internal and external models are dynamic and interdependent; that internal goals have external economic realities; that beliefs can be suspended in certain circumstances; that there are time-variants and time-invariants; that self-sacrifice must be taken into account.

---

[25] Robert Rosen, *Anticipatory Systems: Philosophical, Mathematical, and Methodological Foundations*, Second Edition. New York: Springer. 2012.

If we are to improve upon current "sense and respond" approaches, we need to better understand what models are at work in the broader context of intelligent complex adaptive systems. And much of those models are anticipatory, biological, and sociological, rather than analytical and computational.

Opportunity Disruptor #5: Human-technology integration

Hopefully we've cleared up any lingering concerns you might have had regarding machines taking over the world. Now let's address another ominous scenario currently being discussed. It involves humans and technology eventually becoming one and the same.

There is little doubt that the boundaries between humans and technology are blurring. Processors and other components are being inserted inside the human body, including the brain. Eye movements and hand gestures, and yes, even brain waves are being used as input signals. Some are even saying that eventually you'll be able to tap directly into a large supercomputer as an extension of your own mind.

Human-technology integration is taking place at an ever-faster pace. People who have had their hearing restored through Cochlear implants number in the hundreds of thousands worldwide. RFID chips, first implanted in pets, are now being used by tens of thousands of humans for things like access to public transportation or secure facilities. Forget using your smart phone to pay for things. Just a wave of the hand will suffice. And we are only at the beginning stages.

There's a reason why these types of interfaces are worth pursuing. The human physiology is magnificently equipped with multiple communication modalities. Forty-three muscles produce our facial expressions. Twenty-eight mouth, tongue, and-throat combinations deliver the spoken word, accompanied by literally hundreds of different hand gestures.

These have all served us well, supporting knowledge transfer through stories, music, dance, and other physical forms of expression long before computers ever came along. Now with virtual and augmented reality (VR/AR), including gloves, goggles, contact lenses, body cameras, sensors, and a myriad of other wearable devices, our communication modalities are becoming more experiential and emotionally engaging. Not to mention bringing new hope and dramatic improvements in the quality of life for people with a whole range of challenges and disabilities. This also creates the potential for creating safer and more durable structures, improving our ability to operate in previously inaccessible environments, from the very vast (space) to the very small (nanotechnology). Which brings us to…

Opportunity Disruptor #6: Integrative medicine and increased longevity

What exactly do we mean by "longevity?" If you apply the previous disruptor and upload your memory engrams into the cloud, who knows how long you might be able to "live." From stem cell production to 3-D printing of living tissue and organs (both of which are currently in full swing), the day is coming when you'll be able to order replacements for at least some of your worn-out body parts, much like you do for your car.

As we mentioned earlier, we will certainly encounter *"S-curve"* limitations along the way. But given all the scientific breakthroughs at our disposal today, we still can't systems-engineer even the smallest protozoan from scratch, let alone the entire human physiology. The sooner we realize that there will always be a difference between natural systems and artificial systems, the better. But augmenting one with the other in the right way is both feasible and desirable.

The path to significant life extension might very well be a combination of natural approaches augmented with, but not entirely replaced by, the artificial. Advancements in the fields of integrative medicine, nutrition, and related disciplines such as pharmacogenomics and epigenetics requires building and maintaining (i.e., curating) bodies of knowledge on a massive scale.[26]

The economic potential is huge. How much longer can the consumer-based economy continue to grow? There are only so many gadgets to play with, videos to watch, fantasy leagues and online gaming communities to join.

The next wave will very likely move us away from the virtual and back to the real. This means greatly expanding our awareness. Extending longevity and quality of life. Neutralizing the toxicity and pollution that have accumulated both in our bodies and our environment. And other breakthroughs we haven't even begun to imagine.

For too long we've focused on the advancement of technology while shortchanging human growth and evolution. In our search for artificial intelligence, we've overlooked the most powerful source of intelligence of all: the human physiology (we discuss this later in Chapter 18: *Enough Technology Already, What About Us Humans?*).

We have the opportunity to co-create a sustainable system of integrative medicine that takes into account the human physiology and psychology in all its inherent complexity, as well as our relationship to nature as a whole. Many of those relationships are hidden deep beneath the surface of our observable world. Which brings us to...

---

[26] The George Washington University, which offered the first Pharmacogenomics undergraduate degree program in the U.S., has expanded their offerings to include graduate degrees in Anatomical and Translational Sciences (smhs.gwu.edu/anatomy/education/m-ats).

Opportunity Disruptor #7: Connection to deep structure

You might be wondering: "What exactly is deep structure?" It's like the layers of rock hidden deep beneath the Earth's surface. You know they're there but you can't really see them.

But you can model them. Diagram them. Describe them in various ways, using color, texture, and a host of other attributes.

The same goes for deep knowledge. Deep knowledge resides in two places: in nature's intelligence, and deep in human memory. At what we call the engram level.

And how are these deep structures revealed? We "tease them out" as best we can by a systematic process of thinking, observing, enumerating, expressing, assessing, and adjusting.[27]

All the great thinkers did this. Einstein uncovered many of the deep structures underlying quantum physics when he asked himself: *"What would it be like to ride on a beam of light?"*

Other insights to deep structure come from the work of Robert Rosen, whom we mentioned earlier in Opportunity Disrupter #4, regarding time-variant and time-invariant structures. Just like the earth's massive, slow-moving tectonic plates, the deeper you go, the more time-invariant things tend to become. And just like those tectonic plates, it's *stratified*, as opposed to *continuous*. In the era of big data, with innumerable zettabytes swirling around, it's easy to lose sight of the fact that there are stratified, time-invariant structures at the heart of it all.

At its most fundamental level, deep structure consists of a set of basic elements or *"atoms"* and their *rules of aggregation*. Atoms are another type of basic element. The *periodic table of the elements* exhibits this type of structure. Subject to the natural laws of valence, they can only be

---

[27] This process is spelled out in detail in Arthur J. Murray, *Deep Learning Manual: the knowledge explorer's guide to self-discovery in education, work and life*, Applied Knowledge Sciences Press, 2016.

combined in certain ways. Yet an almost infinite variety of valid combinations are possible.

New compounds continue to emerge from our chemical and metallurgical laboratories almost on a daily basis. But it's the knowledge of deep structure that separates the study of today's chemistry from the study of alchemy in the past.

Deep structure is also present in the relatively small set of phonemes from which all human speech and language is constructed. Root sounds, when combined in ways that are syntactically and semantically correct, make sense. Other combinations which violate the rules of syntax and grammar make no sense. Unless of course, the combination represents a new type of expression, in which case the rules of grammar are modified.

This type of system, in which the underlying rules are occasionally modified based on the introduction of new evidence, is referred to in the knowledge sciences as a *second-order cybernetic system*. It simply means that unlike a first-order system in which the rules are "hard-wired" (such as a simple thermostat or the tax tables in an accounting system), a second-order cybernetic system can self-modify its rules as conditions change. In more advanced systems, the underlying rules can be modified even in anticipation of changes which may occur in the future.

Sadly, this knowledge of deep structure has been lacking as we've amassed our vast human library known as the internet. Such thinking alone can lend a perspective of stability in a world fraught with 20-second sound bites and 140-character tweets.

Here's one more twist to keep in mind. We've mentioned earlier that deep structure is stratified. It consists mainly of nonlinear structures, including multiple quantum states that a single particle can exhibit at the same instant.

For now you don't need to worry much about such properties other than the fact that they exist. Like geology, you know the earth has tectonic plates moving at extremely slow speeds deep beneath the surface. You don't have to actually see them.

But when those plates suddenly slip, causing an earthquake or a tsunami, you are reminded of their presence. So it is with much of our world, including our socio-economic and political systems. In fact, there is an entire sub-discipline known as *event chemistry* which applies the principles of stratification to human behaviors.[28]

Much of this is based on the work of Karl Pribram, whose holonomic model posited a stratified structure in which stable memory elements are formed at the level of conscious awareness (surface learning), while base elements of memory (engrams) exist at a deep level, separated by an epistemic gap.[29] These principles will likely come into play in greater ways as the world continues along its current path of increasing speed of change and complexity.

Looking ahead, here are three areas of opportunity to keep in mind: 1) human deep learning will catch up to machine learning, which will lead to 2) expanded human consciousness (rather than machine consciousness), which will lead to 3) greater ability to see the big picture, with all the key interdependencies.

---

[28] Paul S. Prueitt, *Continuous Analogs to Discrete Dynamical Systems with Application to Modeling Biological Response*, Hampton University, 1989.
[29] Karl Pribram *The Deep and Surface Structure of Memory and Conscious Learning: Toward a 21st Century Model*, Brain Center, Radford University, February 20, 1996.

Opportunity Disruptor #8: Eight billion minds and 100 billion devices

Billions of mobile computing applications are downloaded annually. Combine this with the steadily decreasing unit cost and increasing accessibility of computing resources via the cloud, and ultimately you have a lot of power placed in the hands of just about everyone on the planet. This includes buying power, political power, wealth-generating power, you name it. Only less than a century ago, such power was reserved only for a select few.

But technology advancements are merely enablers. Something much more profound is going on: the blurring of the boundaries separating our living, working and learning environments. This convergence is completely transforming how we interact with the world.

Today's knowledge workers have a boundaryless mindset. The growth of "e-lancing" and other trends show that work is migrating to the worker, rather than vice versa. And knowledge workers are much more discriminating about what they do and for whom they do it.

People can live, work and learn virtually anywhere – at the office, coffee shop, airport lounge or beach house. The bottom line: you as a leader can no longer focus solely on the productivity aspects of your workforce, while ignoring *living* and *learning*. The enterprise of the future must bring all three of these environments into balance.

We've already seen how the cloud enables us to better organize, both physically and virtually. The micro-enterprise of the social knowledge entrepreneur is only one of many different forms of knowledge worker aggregation (see Figure 6-1). For example, knowledge workers and entrepreneurs form communities of practice (CoPs): virtual forums where knowledge is generated, shared, and applied.

```
┌─────────────────────────────────────┐
│        Global Knowledge Economy      │
└─────────────────────────────────────┘
                   ▲
┌─────────────────────────────────────┐
│             Smart Cities             │
└─────────────────────────────────────┘
                   ▲
┌─────────────────────────────────────┐
│    World Trade Centers, Science &    │
│  Technology Parks, and Innovation Clusters │
└─────────────────────────────────────┘
                   ▲
┌───────────────────────────────────────────────┐
│ Knowledge Enterprises, Business Incubators and Accelerators │
└───────────────────────────────────────────────┘
                   ▲
┌──────────────────────────┐        ┌──────────────────┐
│ Knowledge Workers and Social │ ────▶ │ Communities of   │
│  Knowledge Entrepreneurs     │        │    Practice      │
└──────────────────────────┘        └──────────────────┘
```

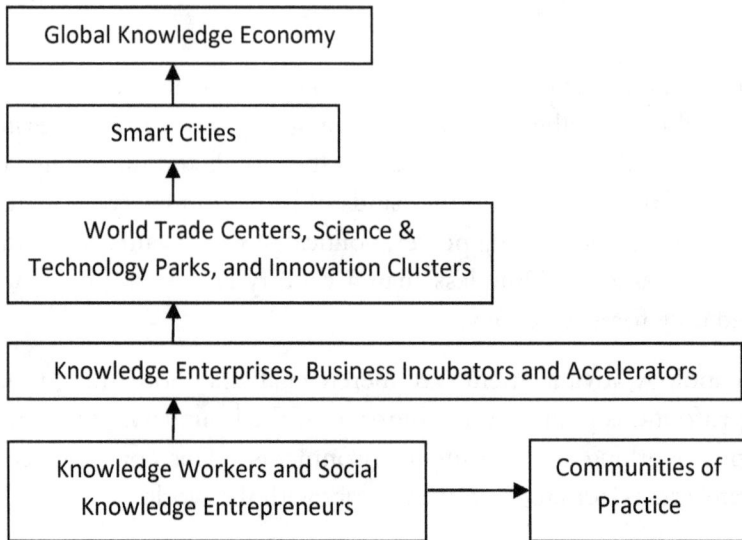

Figure 6-1. Common Forms of Knowledge Worker Aggregation

Knowledge workers may also belong to one or more enterprises, often supported by business incubators and accelerators, which can be government, commercial, or non-profit in nature. Likewise, various knowledge enterprises can choose to co-locate within world trade centers, science and technology parks, and areas of innovation. All three often work together to build a local or regional capability within a major industry such as semiconductors, telecommunications, space systems, biotechnology, or nanotechnology, to name a few. Chapter 21 presents a more detailed illustration of this vision.

Such communities can be expanded further to form what are now being called *smart cities*. These are popping up everywhere, from Helsinki Finland's Kalasatama district, where residents actually initiate, co-develop and test smart city innovations, to Isfahan, Iran, with its two science parks, 10 technology incubators and more than 450 knowledge-based companies.

At the forefront of this trend is a new breed of entrepreneur known as the *social knowledge entrepreneur.* This remarkable individual locates resources online, organizes them, and applies them to fulfill a need. The goal is to deliver the greatest possible benefit to society while rewarding all stakeholders and generating the additional wealth needed to sustain the process.

According to global impact investment advisor Mark Minevich, the social knowledge entrepreneur has the following recognizable traits:

- Challenges the status quo
- Inspires a shared vision and mobilizes the means to affect needed change
- Operates where local, national and global markets cannot, because the financial risks are too great, but seeks those areas because the potential for social impact is the greatest
- Invests in developing global knowledge-based industries and clusters
- Re-tools with new value-added skills and experience to become competitive in the global knowledge economy.[30]

Social knowledge entrepreneurs engage the workforce of the future through new, enlightened approaches to acquiring, developing, nurturing, and growing human talent. This new brand of entrepreneurship combined with responsible investment is essential for a sustainable knowledge economy of billions of minds.

The growing proliferation of electronic payments further enables enterprising individuals to build and grow global knowledge enterprises. And we're talking much more than just online shopping carts using credit cards.

Literally coming from out of nowhere, the internet company Tencent Holdings Ltd., has a market cap of $325B, making it the 10th largest company in the world. It dominates essentially every aspect of internet activity in China, including, most importantly, online payments by

---

[30] Mark D. Minevich, *Billion Minds Foundation: Mission, Goals, Initiatives and Benefits*, May 2007.

mobile devices. In many transactions, a bank isn't even involved. Money just flows from digital wallet to digital wallet. And as we mentioned earlier, the time will come when you won't even need to use your phone. The chip implanted under your skin will do.

From an economic standpoint, we should all be cheering. The emerging climate is as close to perfect competition as we've ever seen in all of human history, characterized by near total transparency, and a level playing field for everyone, with few or no barriers to entry. Under such conditions, work, like money, will quickly flow to where it's treated best. The potential reach is particularly compelling considering the growing market at the "bottom of the pyramid" as originally envisioned by C.K. Prahalad.[31]

As we'll see in Part IV, an enterprise of the future must be attuned to and even take on leadership roles in emerging trends. Groundbreaking strategic advances can result through the convergence of two or more major trends.

One such disruptive opportunity is the convergence of two mature trends (open source and collaborative computing) and a relatively new trend (3-D printing). Here's an example of how it might play out.

Open source. An initial design is created by drawing from a growing library of open source hardware and software. Arduino[32] is one such resource. It's both a programming language and open source hardware platform. It has a wide variety of project templates available for designers and developers to use, copy, modify and enhance. A few examples of existing templates include: an auto-lacing shoe called "Power Laces;" a biking jacket with large, highly visible LED turn signals; a tree-climbing robot; a remote-controlled lawnmower; and perhaps best of all, a chess-playing robot. Of course, knowledge entrepreneurs can create their own projects from scratch if desired.

---

[31] C. K. Prahalad, *The Fortune at the Bottom of the Pyramid: Eradicating Poverty Through Profits*, Wharton School Publishing, 2005.
[32] arduino.cc

<u>Collaborative computing</u>. Innovators can conduct reviews and solicit feedback by participating in one or more maker communities. Participants in these communities number in the millions. *"The Instructables"* is one such community, with over 100,000 open source projects available.

<u>3-D printing</u>. Products are manufactured by assembling and shaping the "atoms" from scratch. And just like any cloud-based resource, the 3-D printers can be located in a shared space. For example, TechShop[33] not only has 3-D printers but also handheld plasma beam cutters and other manufacturing equipment available for rent by the hour at any of their eight locations across the country.

That's only a small sample of what's available. As programming languages and interfaces become more standardized, look for the internet of things to really take off. And for a truly exciting glimpse into the future, check out MIT's *Center for Bits and Atoms,*[34] a maker-based offshoot of the *Media Lab*.

According to IBM, the number of addressable devices will expand by an order of magnitude from its current 10 billion to over 100 billion.[35] With a brain trust of eight billion minds to draw upon, along with all of the software and hardware resources available through the cloud and its connection to tens of billions of devices, you should not feel constrained. Let your imagination run wild. The possibilities are endless.

---

[33] techshop.ws
[34] cba.mit.edu
[35] *Device Democracy: Saving the Future of the Internet of Things*, Executive Report, IBM Institute for Business Value, 2015.

Part IV

A Framework for Continuous Renewal

With academics on one end and practitioners on the other, there seems to be a constant tug-of-war between theory and practice. Theory is necessary because it forms the basis for research and discovery into the laws governing how our world works. Practice is the repeatable application of a theory with the goal of producing predictable results.

Practitioners say, "I don't have time for all this theoretical stuff. Just give me something I can do that will produce real results, starting yesterday." Academics say, "This is nonsense. You haven't proven anything. You need to undergo a rigorous scientific review process before you can claim any of this stuff actually works."

Meanwhile, the tug-of-war goes on. Practitioners who adopt the latest "do's and don'ts" or "seven keys to success" amplify their frustration when "best practices" don't work in their particular situation. Pure theoreticians chastise both groups, arguing that there is no validated theory of the firm, no equivalent of $e=mc^2$ in the field of management.

Despite their shortcomings, frameworks give us a way to bridge the gap between these two worlds. They allow us to organize theories into topics and categories so we can make better sense of how they relate to the real world. Our enterprise of the future framework builds upon a set of principles that have been widely accepted in both academic and professional circles. These are the four conceptual pillars of *leadership, technology, organization,* and *learning,* which we have mapped into the more actionable categories of *leading, connecting, co-creating* and *discovering.*

We've already established that market conditions are changing more rapidly than ever. Frameworks help bring order to the chaos by defining a basic set of foundational elements which remain stable over a longer period of time. When we see a change occurring in the marketplace, we have a reference base we can check. If the underlying framework still holds, we can adjust to the change with a higher degree of confidence. If the framework doesn't hold, we need to modify the theory.

Despite the turmoil of recent years, the four pillars framework has held up reasonably well, as have the underlying principles. In Part IV, we define our framework for the enterprise of the future. This sets the stage for Part V which covers how to make the transition, which in turn provides a solid foundation for understanding the tools and practices presented in Part VI.

Chapter 7

The Enterprise of the Future Defined

One of the more interesting aspects of the enterprise of the future is that it's always evolving. Even though we may be able to anticipate and even co-create the future to some extent, we need to simultaneously keep preparing for the next wave. And the wave after that (recall Figure 3-3).

This demands a totally different type of enterprise. One that is self-aware and highly adaptive. More specifically, as we stated in the Preface and will repeat here:

The Enterprise of the Future is a self-organizing, adaptive, learning network of social knowledge entrepreneurs achieving mutual goals.

By mutual we mean both the individual and the enterprise. Such an enterprise must:

- Quickly learn and adapt to changes in the environment
- Find value where others can't
- Make enlightened business decisions
- Quickly and effectively carry out those decisions
- Measure outcomes and make adjustments
- Continuously innovate – driving the changes in the market rather than vice versa.

The benefits of transitioning to an enterprise of the future are many. Organizations achieve measurable improvements in learning rates, concept-to-development cycle times, and time-to-market. Improved collaboration in a global, virtual environment further improves the ability to respond to, and even create, new opportunities.

Lower labor costs and increased global competitiveness result from improved knowledge worker productivity (working smarter, not harder). Better alignment of work processes, culture, and enterprise architecture yields increased return-on-investment in technology. The enhanced ability to capture, share, apply, and grow key intellectual assets allows organizations to maintain or increase their relative strength in market valuation.

Improved learning and better decision-making results in reduced risk, along with reduced costs and liability due to errors. Streamlined, rapidly self-organizing collaborative processes improve the capacity of organizations to quickly respond to and even drive change. Productivity gains help keep labor costs competitive, with equal or better quality and performance.

Traditional organizations need to evolve to a new level in order to realize these benefits. Table 7-1 lists key attributes that characterize the transition from a traditional organization to a next-generation enterprise.

Table 7-1. Key differences between traditional organizations and an enterprise of the future

Traditional organizations:		Future enterprises:
Hierarchies	→	Networks
Authoritarian leaders	→	Knowledge-enabling leaders
Silos	→	Open spaces
The individual worker	→	Individuals, teams and communities
Knowledge hoarding	→	Knowledge co-creation and sharing
Slow, random learning	→	Rapid, double-loop learning
Repeating mistakes	→	Learning from past mistakes and proactively avoiding future mistakes
Reactive	→	Anticipatory
Point fixes	→	Systemic solutions
Hindsight	→	Foresight
Mass/niche markets	→	Massive customization
Make-sell	→	Co-create
Presentations	→	Conversations
Re-inventing the wheel (redundant effort)	→	Inventing entirely new paradigms
Quarterly revenues and profits	→	Sustained value generation
Saying: *"That'll never work here"*	→	Saying: *"Let's find a way to make it work."*
Asking: *"How many employees do we have?"*	→	Asking: *"How do we draw from a talent pool of billions of minds located anywhere on the planet?"*

While few if any enterprises will exhibit mastery over all of the above attributes, each needs to be present at least to some degree. You can use the following short list of goals as you plan and implement the transition of your organization to a knowledge-based enterprise of the future:

- Embedding rapid innovation and learning deep in the organization's core work processes
- Harnessing the integration of communities and teams to quickly transfer knowledge when and where it's needed
- Uncovering and leveraging hidden capabilities
- Rewarding knowledge-sharing in a highly competitive environment
- Providing a personalized, highly productive work environment where information seamlessly follows workers wherever they go
- Building and maintaining a work environment which attracts, retains and grows the best and brightest performers
- Understanding and applying the notion of co-creating the future
- Identifying measurable ways for knowledge workers and entrepreneurs to increase the value of their work.

Legacy institutions are ill-equipped to keep pace with the changes in the global marketplace. To be clear, we're not proposing doing away with such organizations. But we are proposing to transform how we organize ourselves far beyond traditional boundaries and structures.

For example, legacy institutions have become hopelessly bogged down in paperwork, inertia, and fear of making mistakes to the point where they can barely do their current work, let alone anticipate and provide for future needs. In an enterprise of the future, business agreements and contracts still exist, but they are put in-place ahead of time in order to improve the ability to create and/or respond to "pop-up" opportunities. More importantly, they are simple and written in plain English.

The Enterprise of the Future Framework

The concept of the enterprise of the future is built upon a theoretical framework that draws from over a decade of university-level research. The framework consists of four primary facets or pillars, illustrated in Figure 7-1. These four pillars are briefly described below and in greater depth in Chapters 8-11. A quick-reference summary is provided in Appendix A.

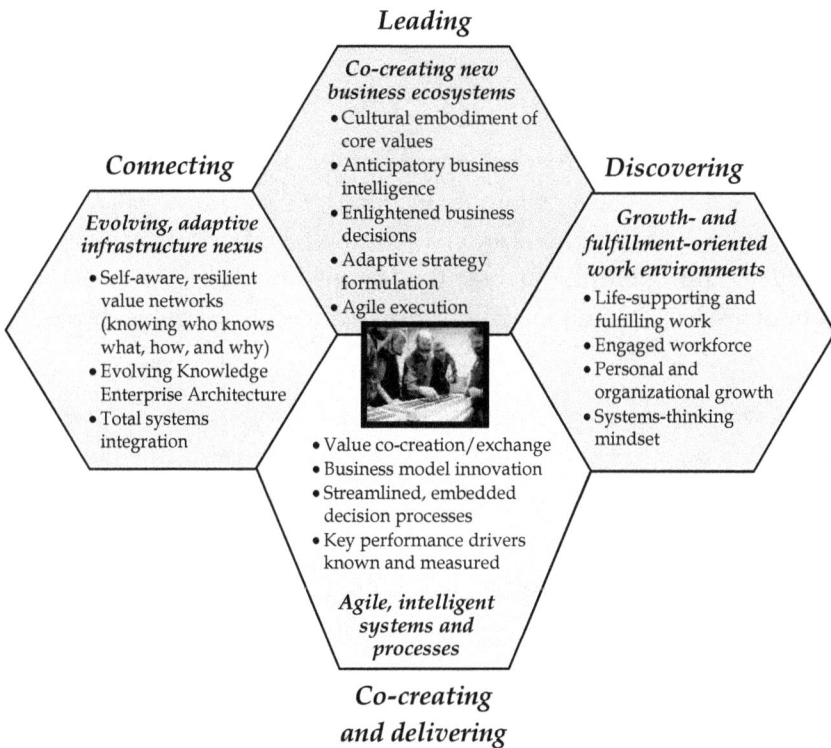

Leading

Co-creating new business ecosystems
- Cultural embodiment of core values
- Anticipatory business intelligence
- Enlightened business decisions
- Adaptive strategy formulation
- Agile execution

Connecting

Evolving, adaptive infrastructure nexus
- Self-aware, resilient value networks (knowing who knows what, how, and why)
- Evolving Knowledge Enterprise Architecture
- Total systems integration

Discovering

Growth- and fulfillment-oriented work environments
- Life-supporting and fulfilling work
- Engaged workforce
- Personal and organizational growth
- Systems-thinking mindset

- Value co-creation/exchange
- Business model innovation
- Streamlined, embedded decision processes
- Key performance drivers known and measured

Agile, intelligent systems and processes

Co-creating and delivering

Figure 7-1. Enterprise of the Future Conceptual Framework

Leading

Building the enterprise of the future means completely rethinking strategy, even to the point of co-creating entirely new business ecosystems. Transforming the very structures of society, whether technological, economic, or political, is not out of the question.

Strategy cannot be formulated in a vacuum. At the same time, vision cannot be conceived without knowledge and insights into trends which will shape and impact the strategy. Predicting and tracking major trends in the marketplace and aligning strategy with those trends allows organizations not only to predict, but also to co-create, the future. In this way, organizations are better able to confront reality in a world that is growing more "virtual" every day.

Connecting

Let's face it. Connecting billions of minds and tens of billions of devices cannot occur without technology, or more specifically, Information and Communication Technology (ICT). Still, we need to carefully and vigilantly avoid the temptation to leap ahead to technology-based solutions without first considering people, business processes, and especially, strategy.

We view technology as an enabler. Our goal with respect to this pillar is to stitch together many disparate internal and external components into an evolving, adaptive, self-aware *infrastructure nexus*.

Companies that can build such a nexus will be able to capture and retain critical knowledge efficiently and effectively, thereby attracting and retaining the next generation of workers. A highly productive workforce means greater satisfaction, less time wasted, and increased output with the same staffing levels.

Co-creating and delivering extraordinary value

For the enterprise of the future, one of the central themes is organizing for sustained high performance in a non-hierarchical world. Industrial age, even information age structures are inadequate for achieving this goal. By structures we mean not only the traditional organization chart, but also the processes, social networks, ontology, and most importantly, the business model itself.

Hierarchies and matrices need to be replaced by fluid, agile, social networks and communities. Process models can no longer focus solely on tasks, but must include streamlined decision flows. In the compressed time cycles of today's world, the right decisions need to be made quickly and consistently at points dispersed from central authority. This demands coming up with entirely new decision models, supported by real-time collaboration tools and self-organizing networking environments.

The main intent is to organize all the resources and assets at the enterprise's disposal in a way that consistently delivers timely, relevant knowledge and experience to the key decision points in a business process. In other words, to apply the enterprise's collective know-how when and where it's needed. All aimed, of course, at co-creating sustained extraordinary value for the customer.

Making breakthrough discoveries

Much of the value of an organization, typically eighty percent or more, ultimately lives or dies within this pillar. As a result, new valuation methods, in which individual and organizational knowledge is created, shared, measured, and nurtured, need to be developed.

People form the core of any enterprise. As a consequence, innovating, learning, and transforming at least as fast as, or faster than, the speed of change in your market demands both an individual and organizational perspective. New competency development and motivational systems are needed to attract, retain, and grow the world's best social knowledge entrepreneurs and workers. This in turn provides an environment with abundant opportunities for personal and organizational performance, growth and achievement.

Chapter 8

Leading

<u>Key roles</u>: Chairman; CEO; Executive Director.

<u>Ownership of</u>: Vision; mission; goals; strategy; governance.

<u>Primary focus</u>: Co-creating new business ecosystems and strategies.

<u>Key attributes</u>: Cultural embodiment of core values; anticipatory business intelligence; enlightened business decisions; adaptive strategy formulation; agile execution.

John Maxwell says it best: *"Everything rises and falls on leadership."* Leadership defines the vision, mission, goals, and strategy. Leaders are held accountable for achieving mission success. They also set the tone for what defines the culture of the enterprise.

An organization cannot be agile and adaptive without strong leaders who have the ability to observe and even anticipate changes in the competitive environment. They must be able to quickly formulate strategies for responding to those changes. And they must provide the clarity and drive needed for rapid follow-through and successful execution of those strategies. Ideally, leadership should always be stretching the traditional boundaries of the enterprise, co-creating entirely new business ecosystems if necessary.

Leadership is responsible for strategic alignment throughout the enterprise. In today's fast-changing economy there is little tolerance for various units of an organization moving in different directions. Clear communication and wholesale adoption of vision and mission, goals and strategy is a top priority. Of course the availability of resources across the enterprise needs to be taken into account or the strategy will not be executable.

Table 8-1 lists five key areas on which you as a leader need to focus in order to formulate and execute a coherent and competitive strategy.

Cultural embodiment of core values

This means being able to stay focused on doing the right things in the right way. Turbulent conditions can create a sense of panic, causing organizations to deviate from the principles upon which they were originally founded.

As we reinvent the enterprise, we need to bring core values front and center. Every enterprise needs a clearly defined set of values-based criteria for making strategic and tactical decisions in a manner consistent with the legal, moral and ethical principles under which the organization operates.

We explore this principle further in Chapter 19

Anticipatory Business Intelligence

Being agile and adaptive begins with possessing superior business intelligence (BI). This means not only having the right information, but determining the right course of action to take in response to that information. This is what truly distinguishes a knowledge-era enterprise from an information- or industrial-age enterprise.

Table 8-1. Co-creating new business ecosystems and strategies

Focus Areas:	You'll know you're there when:
Cultural embodiment of core values	Foundational legal, moral and ethical principles under which the organization operates are known and form the basis for decisions made at every level
Anticipatory business intelligence	Data-driven analytics are augmented with biological/social/behavior-driven models
Enlightened business decisions	Business decisions consistently take financial, ethical, societal and environmental stewardship into account
Adaptive strategy formulation	The process for formulating, planning and executing strategy is understood and practiced
	Theory of change is a key part of strategic forecasting and strategy formulation
Agile execution	Master strategy and sub-strategies are clear to everyone and are refined as conditions change
	Everything the organization does is aligned with strategy
	Performance is measured and tracked
	Innovation and learning occur simultaneously

An enterprise of the future must be able to quickly sense, anticipate, and respond to changes in the competitive environment. This cannot be accomplished effectively without anticipatory business intelligence systems that incorporate predictive analytics and anticipatory models.

Note that we use a broad definition of business intelligence which includes both internal and external factors. Predicting and tracking major trends in the marketplace and aligning strategy with those trends within the core capabilities of the enterprise provides the means not only to predict but also to co-create the future. In this way, organizations are better able to confront reality in a world that is growing more uncertain every day.

BI tools analyze large volumes of internal and external data, identify patterns and generate other information useful for making business decisions regarding strategy, product/service development, and process improvement. Each is critical to maintaining competitive advantage.

Anticipatory Business Intelligence means being able to spot trends early and leap ahead conceptually in order to be ready to act as the trend gains momentum. This includes effectively using strategic forecasting and scenario-based planning tools along with digital dashboards to link capabilities with performance.

Clockspeed once again comes into play. The speed and effectiveness of decisions in these key areas determine whether your enterprise is falling behind, keeping pace, or leading the changes in your target market.

Enlightened business decisions

Reaching a peak level of organizational performance means that leadership must have the capacity for making enlightened business decisions. By enlightened we mean decision-making with as broad a view as possible, looking across the entire social, environmental, and economic spectrum. This is in direct opposition to the more familiar pattern of focusing on one or two numbers month-to-month or quarter-to-quarter.

A primary challenge in this regard is balancing effectiveness and efficiency. Effectiveness responds to the need to take financial, ethical, societal and environmental aspects into consideration. Efficient processes aid in making collaborative decisions in ever-shortening time frames.

According to a study of over four hundred organizations, nearly half of all business decisions fail.[36] Two of the main reasons given were premature commitments, and a preponderance of failure-prone

---

[36] Paul C. Nutt, *Why Decisions Fail*, Berrett-Koehler Publishers, 2002.

practices. In the current era of compressed time cycles, the tendency to prematurely rush to judgment only tends to make matters worse. Gartner estimates that more than 35 percent of the top 5,000 global companies will regularly fail to make insightful decisions regarding significant changes in their business and markets.[37]

In the industrial age, and even into the information age, business decisions were just that – business decisions. They were based primarily upon what made the most business sense. For the most part this meant *return-on-investment (ROI)*.

In today's climate a decision must not only make good business sense, but must also be socially acceptable, environmentally sustainable, compatible with principles of good governance, and compliant with thousands of pages of obscure government regulations.

In order to make sound decisions quickly at this level of complexity, you need a system which not only gives decision makers accurate, relevant, and timely information, but also aids in the correct interpretation of that information. This means applying a consistent and well understood decision process, linked to an equally clear understanding of the mission and strategy of the enterprise. Only in this way can you hope to improve your ability to make better strategic decisions in a rapidly changing world.

Adaptive strategy formulation

This area focuses on developing the capacity for quickly sensing, anticipating, and responding to changes in the competitive environment. Although it may seem contradictory, an adaptive strategy requires formalized processes for formulation, planning and execution. Links to strategy and performance are well-defined, monitored and adjusted as needed. The goal here is moving beyond *"sense-and-respond"* to a more anticipatory posture.

---

[37] Gartner Business Intelligence Summit, The Hague, Netherlands, 20-22 January 2009.

We define strategy as the guiding principles which define how the enterprise will meet its top-level goals and objectives and achieve its mission. Strategy used to be synonymous with "long-term." In the last century, strategic plans spanning several decades were not uncommon. But as industry clockspeeds began to accelerate, planning horizons contracted. Today it's not uncommon for an enterprise to revisit its strategy annually, and even more frequently, if necessary.

A strategic plan is similar to a game plan in sports. It defines the opening moves. Then the other side adjusts, weather conditions change, injuries and penalties mount, and the leader spends the remainder of the game making adjustments. Agility in changing strategic direction can only occur in organizations where communications are clear and timely, and localized goals are closely aligned with strategic goals.

A business strategy must flow downward logically and intuitively from the vision, mission, goals and objectives. This flow-down process will be covered later in Chapter 12.

Hopefully the need for strategic alignment is clear. A low-price sales strategy may not be compatible with a highly compressed product development cycle. Aggressive sales growth targets may not be achievable without an equally aggressive acquisition strategy, which in turn may not be achievable without access to large pools of investment capital. Interest rate fluctuations may present risk and may not support a low-price high-volume product mix. In reality, this type of analysis extends much deeper, touching virtually every element within and across the value network. This leads to the next facet of leadership: *agile execution.*

Agile execution

Even if a sound strategy is formulated, the greatest challenge comes in execution. This requires combining the previous four attributes in a way that allow continuous adjustments to be made as conditions change. These changes are often *reflexive* in nature, as competitors introduce counter-strategies and tactics. Knowledge of the resources an enterprise has at its disposal, along with the ability to quickly re-allocate and re-deploy those resources is essential.

The many challenges leadership faces in a complex fast-changing world can be summed up as follows: 1) to formulate a strategy that can be executed in an amorphous, networked enterprise in which there may be conflicting priorities among the individual components; 2) to be able to quickly adjust the strategy and its execution in response to, and even ahead of, changes in the market.

Formulating the right strategy means very little if its execution is flawed. Office files are stuffed with strategic plans, operating plans, and the like. All have been carefully reviewed and signed off by people up, down, and across the organization. Yet all too often, very little ends up according to plan. There are two main reasons for this.

First: *the way events unfold is always unpredictable.* This is true in war, sports, business, and chess. Most plans, including the most carefully thought-out war plans, game plans, and business plans, are valid only for the opening moves. In reality, business situations are highly complex, involving human judgment and many other variables we can neither predict nor control. No strategy can account for all possibilities and variables. A strategic plan serves only as a guide to make sure the right elements are in place at the outset.

Second: *plans set the initial conditions; execution takes it from there.* Plans are static. Execution is dynamic. Plans are based on past experience. Execution occurs in the present moment. This is why human judgment, expertise and decision making are the most crucial elements in successfully executing a business strategy.

The challenge is to build an enterprise that combines depth of information with streamlined decision processes that apply the right information in the right way. We call such decision processes *knowledge*.

Human behavior, based upon past experience, culture and behavior, usually means the difference between a successful or failed strategy.

Although you can never achieve 100% assurance that every decision will have no adverse consequences, you can minimize the chances of their occurrence by achieving what we call strategic alignment throughout the enterprise.

Clearly, if the majority (often 70 to 80 percent) of an organization's asset value is made up of intangible assets, then its performance over the long run will depend upon how well it manages those assets. In order to manage those assets properly, their link to performance must be known and understood.

For example, if an organization chooses a product innovation strategy, it needs to first identify the key performance drivers (e.g., rapid concept-to-market cycles). Next, the underlying core capabilities needed to achieve that level of performance (e.g., tightly integrated value chain management from R&D through design, manufacturing, supply chain logistics, marketing, sales and support) must be fully engaged. Finally, and the processes for managing the critical intellectual assets which enable rapid innovation and learning must be up and running.

Sustained dynamic execution at this level of performance requires superior knowledge. In the next chapter, we'll take a look at how you can enable the smooth flow of knowledge needed to make more timely, consistent and correct business decisions.

Chapter 9

Connecting

<u>Key roles</u>: CIO; CTO; Security Director; Facilities Director.

<u>Ownership of</u>: Enterprise Architecture; external interfaces; information assurance; all aspects of security.

<u>Primary focus</u>: Evolving, adaptive infrastructure nexus.

<u>Key attributes</u>: Self-aware, resilient value networks (knowing who knows what, how, and why); evolving Knowledge Enterprise Architecture; total systems integration.

In an enterprise of the future, the heart of connecting lies in building a self-aware, evolving infrastructure nexus that enables the efficient and effective contribution of the other three pillars. The key word here is *enables*.

Of the four pillars, *connecting* may be the one that experiences the greatest amount of disruption as we look toward the future. Much of our information infrastructure is built upon outmoded, data-centric models. Most legacy databases apply the relational model, even though the majority of the world's knowledge uses a network form of representation. Vast warehouses of data exist with very little, if any, context. These approaches simply will not work in a complex, fast-moving world in which decision-making is extremely situational, contextual, and highly reflexive.

The underlying models are not the only problem. Mismatches occur at all levels, from the organization's vision and mission, all the way down to its core processes, and the people who execute those processes. We need to move beyond the practice of simply delivering information to one of enabling decisions.

The mindset of getting the right information to the right person at the right time is deeply entrenched. Yet we keep hearing that we are "drowning in information and starved for knowledge." Bill Jensen provides an excellent illustration of this problem, in which a mid-level manager in a services company tells him, "All the plans, spreadsheets and milestones…just tell me what's due when. I still don't have what I need that tells me how to get it done."[38] Author John Lewis would add that *why* something needs to be done in the first place is often missing as well.[39]

If, despite the widespread availability of information, half of all business decisions fail, then clearly something is wrong. Our work has shown repeatedly that we need to take another step beyond acquiring and presenting information. We need to assist the decision maker in properly interpreting that information, and in determining the appropriate course of action to take. This cycle of anticipate-observe-interpret-decide-act needs to be fully supported by technology in order to build a true *"just-ahead-of-time"* organization.

---

[38] Bill Jensen, *Simplicity: the new competitive advantage in a world of more, better, faster*, Perseus Books, 2000, p. 13.
[39] John Lewis, *The Explanation Age*, 3rd edition, 2013.

Tight integration across both internal and external components of an enterprise requires a well-defined enterprise architecture. Rapid change is not possible if there are gaps between the organizational and infrastructure elements spanning business models, information and knowledge flows, human capital, pricing considerations, finance and accounting, physical plant and equipment, and intellectual property protection. All of the elements of an enterprise, which have typically operated under their own separate processes and systems, need to perform as an integrated whole. That cannot be accomplished without a unifying architecture. This may very well be the most daunting challenge in building an enterprise of the future.

Table 9-1 lists the key attributes which characterize a future enterprise from the information technology (connecting) perspective.

Self-aware, resilient value networks (knowing who knows what, how and why)

Many organizations don't even have a good handle on who knows what, let alone *how* everything works, the *value* each person brings to the table, and *why*. These are the core elements of a value network.

While social network analysis typically reveals who is talking about what, *value network analysis* aims to reveal the hidden "why's" behind the conversations. In other words, value networks enhance the generation and transfer of value across the many social networks present both internally and externally.[40] Understanding and bringing these value exchanges into the open results in increased participation in communities of practice. Making the network "self-aware" means maximizing transparency, a large part of which is *minimizing the trust footprint*, as we will discuss later in Chapter 20.

---

[40] Verna Allee, *Value network analysis and value conversion of tangible and intangible assets*, Journal of Intellectual Capital, Vol. 9 Issue: 1, p.5-24.

Table 9-1. Evolving, adaptive infrastructure nexus

Focus Areas:	You'll know you're there when:
Self-aware, resilient value networks (knowing who knows *what, how* and *why*)	The network "sees itself," knows *who* knows *what*, and the value each person brings to the table
	Social/Value Network Analysis is practiced and applied
	Self-organization is encouraged and supported
	People actively participate in global knowledge-sharing communities; organizational boundaries are minimized
	Techniques for successful virtual collaboration are practiced and refined
	The right expertise can be easily tapped when needed
	The organization not only knows what it knows, but also "grows what it knows"
	Open communication and the free flow of knowledge across the enterprise are encouraged and enabled
	The capacity for identifying, resisting, absorbing and restoring business operations following a major adverse event is maintained and continuously upgraded
Evolving Knowledge Enterprise Architecture	An Enterprise Architecture which aligns technology with business processes, performance drivers, and strategy, is established and maintained
	Formal tool selection processes are in-place and coordinated
	Technology infrastructure provides ease of access while maximizing privacy and security
Total systems integration	Key components across the enterprise are woven together into a "self-aware" system of systems
	Balance exists between localization and centralization; local systems are seamlessly connected into an integrated whole

In addition, tomorrow's value networks need to be not only robust but also extremely *resilient*. We view resilience as: *the capacity to resist, absorb, and recover from an adverse event.* Note that adverse events cover a wide range including, as we like to say, things that go *bang* (physical threats), things that go *dark* (cyber threats), and things that go *boing* (socio-economic threats).

We've frequently observed that the global knowledge economy is increasingly made up of massive interconnections and consequently, massive interdependencies. There's no such thing as a supply chain anymore. It's a *value web*.

The good news is with its multiple paths and redundancies, a web can be extremely resilient. By the same token it can also be highly vulnerable. Very few business sectors operate in isolation. They need each other. As a result, the whole system can come crashing down as soon as some unknown tipping point is reached.

Whether it be earthquakes or exotic man-made catastrophes such as bio-terror and cyber-attacks, all have the potential for causing protracted (several months or longer) interruption in the flow of basic goods and services. Such a disruption would be an economic disaster for any enterprise, and could quickly spread throughout various sectors of the economy.

For this reason, achieving economic resilience is critical. All the dots need to be connected, which in turn requires a clear understanding of the many interdependencies present.

Evolving knowledge enterprise architecture

Operating as an enterprise of the future means having a full grasp of your enterprise architecture, along with the strengths, weaknesses, and interdependencies among its various components. This includes:

- Establishing and maintaining a formal enterprise architecture and sub-architectures (business, technical, security, etc.) with clearly defined links across technology, strategy, processes, people, competencies, and organizational performance

- Developing guidelines and principles for information governance (e.g., accountability, operational support, content life cycle management)
- Understanding the performance impacts and tradeoffs of security policy and regulatory compliance
- Developing logical and service-oriented architectures which allow freedom and flexibility for agile development, including on-the-fly mashups and mobile applications.

Total systems integration

Despite the widespread adoption of enterprise software platforms and the like, the level of integration needed for high-speed, anticipatory planning and response in complex, rapidly changing environments has not yet been reached. In some instances, the proliferation of technology has only resulted in added chaos and confusion, with little or no gain in productivity.

One reason for this gap is the misalignment of technology investment with business strategy, work processes, intellectual assets, and organizational performance. By viewing the enterprise from a total systems perspective, and leveraging the latest advances in business process modeling and management, an enterprise of the future seeks to "stitch" together the various organizational elements, processes, and enabling technologies. This enables the seamless flow of knowledge, resulting in continuous innovation and learning, and sustainable increases in organizational performance. Balance must exist between localization and centralization. Local systems must be seamlessly connected into an integrated whole

The goal here is to build one seamless, secure environment for managing individual and organizational knowledge, and enhancing productivity, regardless of location (home, office, or mobile).

Chapter 10

Co-Creating and Delivering Extraordinary Value

<u>Key roles</u>: COO; CMO; CFO.

<u>Ownership of</u>: Business models, systems and processes; KPIs (key performance indicators).

<u>Primary focus</u>: Agile, intelligent systems and processes.

<u>Key attributes</u>: Value co-creation/exchange; business model innovation; streamlined, embedded decision processes; key performance drivers known and measured.

Of the many changes we've been witnessing in the transition to a global knowledge economy, the very notions of "job" and "work" are rapidly becoming obsolete. At least in the traditional sense.

We define *work* as the activity that needs to occur in order to produce a specific result. *Work processes* are repeatable models of that activity. The activity can be performed by humans, machines, or both.

An enterprise of the future seeks the most efficient and effective aggregation of people, work processes, and automation which consistently delivers the best results. And results are measured by the *value* they bring less the total costs of co-creating and delivering that value.

That said, work (all of the tasks and activities associated with co-creating, delivering, receiving and growing extraordinary value) still needs to be organized in some way.

Organizations have been experiencing a seemingly never-ending conflict between the old guard hierarchy and the brave new world of social networks. Management texts going back 50 years or more have recognized the existence of both the formal and informal organization. These two worlds co-existed peacefully for the most part, when industry clock speeds were measured in years.

That clearly is no longer the case. The massive global proliferation of low cost communications has enabled workers to bypass the old command and control hierarchy. Even traditional hierarchical organizations such as the U.S. Armed Services have had to massively delegate decision-making authority down to the lowest levels, where tactical intelligence is shared with ground forces who act on that intelligence nearly instantaneously.

We mentioned earlier that much of the value of the 21st century organization lies within intangible assets such as intellectual capital. Aside from formal patents and other more explicit forms of knowledge, most of this intellectual capital resides in the form of personal "know-how" and experience, often referred to as *tacit knowledge*.

To the extent that this knowledge is shared or transferred, it usually takes place within social networks – the communities to which knowledge workers belong. In an enterprise of the future, this is where most of the value resides. Leaders of the 21st century need to support the self-organizing emergence, cultivation and proliferation of knowledge networks within and across their organizations.

The design of the next-generation enterprise should enable the seamless flow of timely, relevant knowledge and experience to key nodes within its value network. This helps bring an organization's collective know-how to bear when and where it's needed.

The difference between the old and new forms of organization is illustrated in Figure 10-1 below. Key attributes supporting value co-creation and delivery are summarized in Table 10-1.

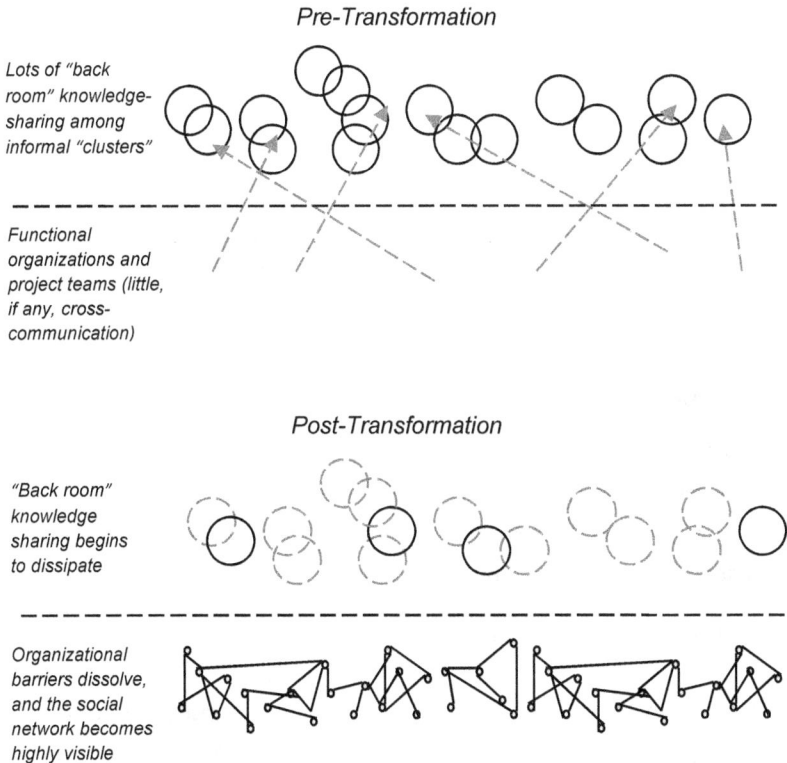

Figure 10-1. Bringing the informal network out of the shadows

Table 10-1. Agile, intelligent systems and processes

Focus Areas:	You'll know you're there when:
Value co-creation/exchange	The value of tangible and intangible assets is known and tracked
	Value gaps and opportunities are quickly identified and quantified
Business model innovation	All aspects of the business model are measured and evaluated on a regular basis
	New means for exchanging value are developed and tested on a regular basis
Streamlined, embedded decision processes	Innovation and learning occur more by design than by chance
	The knowledge life cycle is an integral part of all work and decision processes
	The entire workforce understands, expects, promotes and manages change
Key performance drivers known and measured	Industry clockspeed is known and compared to internal development cycles
	Underlying core capabilities needed to achieve the desired level of performance are understood and managed

Value co-creation and delivery

The whole purpose of an enterprise is to *co-create, deliver, receive and grow extraordinary value on a sustained basis.* We say extraordinary because in a world in which the barriers to entry continue to dissolve, success means rising above the competition by delivering *outstanding* results.

This is contrary to old-school thought, which teaches that the purpose of an enterprise is to maximize shareholder value. Having profit as the major criterion for success is like saying that one's purpose in life is to breathe and circulate blood. Of course an enterprise needs to make money, just as a person needs to breathe and perform other vital functions.

In the enterprise of the future, we take a much broader view. Instead of profit, at the very least you should be thinking *EVA*, or *economic value added*. This means creating monetary value that exceeds the opportunity cost of capital. Better yet, your view of business success should consider the triple bottom line (TBL) of economic, societal, and environmental benefits.

Clearly, money is no longer the sole medium of value exchange. Mergers and acquisitions are performed based on exchanges of shares of stock, the value of which may be entirely based on the contents of each firm's intellectual property portfolio. Or its brand.

There are many ways of determining value. Value, like money itself, is treated based on market perception and a number of other factors, not the least of which is supply and demand. Market distortions aside, even the closing prices of currencies, stocks, commodities and the like are based heavily on the perceived value assigned by the market. Which is why intangible assets come into play so heavily.

Take the examples we've seen in Internet-based companies. In the decade of the 1990's, valuations based on clicks went through the roof only to return crashing down to earth. Clicks have high value one day and are worthless the next.

The same cycle is likely being repeated with platforms such as *WhatsApp*, which was acquired by *Facebook* for $19B, or about $40 per user. At the time of this writing, *Facebook* has roughly 2 billion users, with a market valuation just south of half a trillion dollars.

One of the best ways to co-create value is to find out what customers want, then find a way to provide it at a total cost of ownership that is significantly less than the return those customers will receive. This is why addressing the entire cycle of co-creating, delivering, receiving and growing value is far more important than just trying to answer the question *"how much money are we making?"*

This means getting everything you can from both your tangible and intangible assets, with emphasis on the intangible. The key to success is gaining the ability to quickly identify and quantify gaps and opportunities that can increase value for the enterprise, its clients, partners and stakeholders.

The process of identifying and responding to gaps and opportunities is the basis of innovation. Next we'll take a look at an area that is ripe for innovation, but often neglected – the *business model*.

Business model innovation

Business models are functional descriptions of how an enterprise co-creates, delivers, receives and grows extraordinary value. Old business models were based on a *make-sell strategy*. Most of today's have more of a *sense-and-respond* flavor.

The third and latest approach is more anticipatory, in which all stakeholders, clients and suppliers co-create the future by looking ahead and working back, rather than the opposite. We've been referring to this as *just-ahead-of-time*.

Enterprises should expect to see their business models change approximately once every three years. The models themselves become a part of the ever-changing and evolving competitive landscape.

One of the more notable examples has been *Amazon's* ongoing disruption of entire industries, the latest being how we will purchase groceries and other household items in the future. Its acquisition of organic food chain *Whole Foods*, combined with *AmazonGo*, delivery drones, and its cloud-based machine-learning platform, comprise a formidable arsenal of transformational capability.

Streamlined, embedded decision processes

For too long, knowledge has been separated from work. From the old industrial age admonition "I don't pay you to think" to modern-day notions of *explicit* vs. *tacit*, knowledge has always been treated as something intangible and consequently unmanageable.

In order to meet the demands of fast innovation and learning, the enterprise of the future has no choice but to bring these two worlds of knowledge and work together. The way to do this is to make the steps of capturing, sharing, applying and growing knowledge an embedded, permanent part of key work processes (see Figure 10.2).

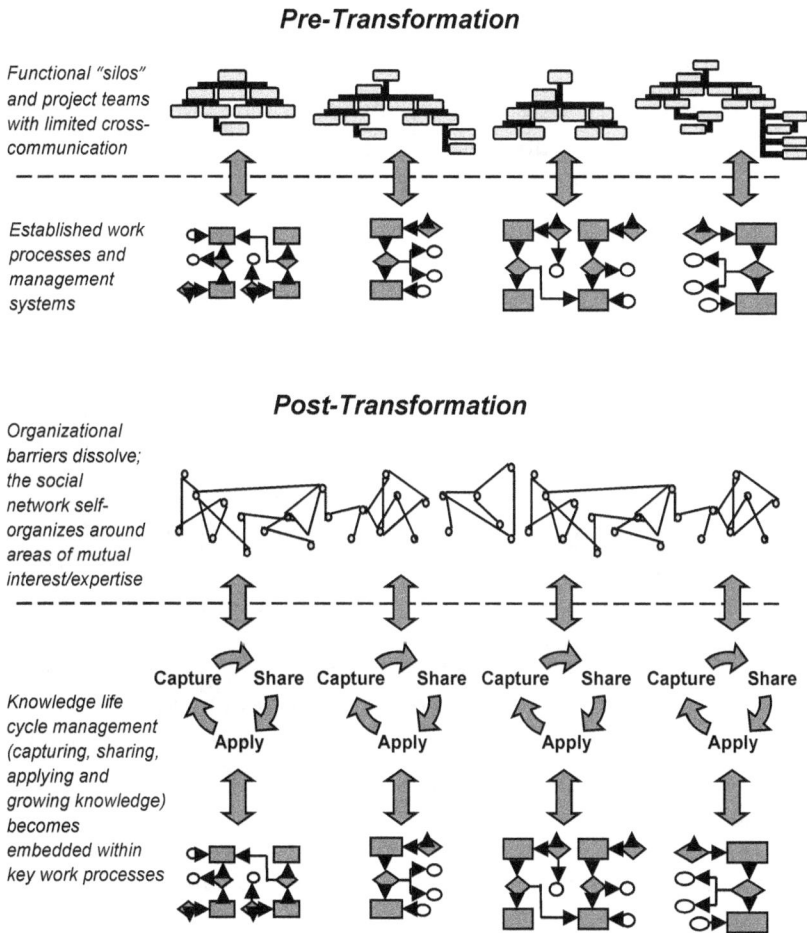

Figure 10-2. Embedding the knowledge life cycle within key work processes

This means process models can no longer focus only on tasks, but must include streamlined processes for making decisions. In the compressed time cycles of today's world, the right decisions need to be made quickly and consistently at points dispersed from central authority. This requires entirely new decision-making models, supported by real-time collaboration tools and self-organizing networking environments.

People throughout the enterprise need to apply large volumes of structured and unstructured data and information to making informed, consistent decisions. By organizing and integrating the vast assortment of infrastructure elements (discussed in Chapter 9), coupled with best practices, your enterprise will be on a path of continuous discovery of new ways to boost workforce performance on all levels.

Key performance drivers known and measured

Your organization's performance drivers are the primary factors that make the difference between success and failure in achieving your strategic goals and objectives. For example, if your mission is speed-oriented, such as *"absolutely, positively by 10:00 am,"* or *"delivered in 30 minutes or it's free,"* then your performance drivers should be speed-oriented as well. In this case, the performance demands will be focused on the logistics of preparation, packaging, and delivery.

Likewise, if your primary marketing message is *"if you are dissatisfied for any reason, return the product for a full refund,"* then your major performance drivers will tend to be quality-oriented. A low-price strategy such as Wal-Mart's places huge performance demands on supply-chain systems.

Knowledge-intensive companies develop performance criteria based on improving their decision processes. Four common decision criteria are: 1) time-to-decision; 2) cost-of-decision; 3) quality-of-decision; 4) capacity-for-decision (i.e., decision throughput).[41]

---

[41] Developed by David Bromberg of the Soifer Center, White Plains, NY.

Other examples of performance drivers include:

- Consistency
- Efficiency
- Accuracy
- Responsiveness
- Cost control
- Reliability
- Availability
- Asset utilization
- Superior technical support.

It all boils down to prioritizing what's most important. However, be careful not to focus on only a few key drivers in isolation. Organizations are inherently complex, and many performance drivers in one area have interdependencies impacting other areas of the enterprise. For example, cutting overhead expenses such as rent and office furnishings may cause a momentary bump in profits, but the long-term effects may result in reduced morale and productivity.

While many performance drivers tend to be customer-oriented, some organizations place the greatest emphasis on their employees. The Virgin Group, for example, believes that if employees are happy and fulfilled in their work, their attitudes will naturally translate into excellent customer service, resulting in happy customers. This also results in increased brand recognition, business growth, and profitability.

Chapter 11

Making Breakthrough Discoveries

<u>Key roles</u>: CKO, CLO, VP R&D.

<u>Ownership of</u>: Intellectual asset portfolio; innovation-and-learning growth cycle.

<u>Primary focus</u>: Growth- and fulfillment-oriented work environments.

<u>Key attributes</u>: Life-supporting and fulfilling work; engaged workforce; personal and organizational growth; systems-thinking mindset.

Breakthrough discoveries don't happen without people. And not just any people. You need the right people, with the right mindset, in the right cultural environment.

This is why a culture instilled with a desire for rapid innovation, learning and growth is at the core of the enterprise of the future framework. This means attracting, retaining, and growing adaptive, innovative leaders and knowledge entrepreneurs. It means knowing what such individuals want and creating an environment in which their goals and those of the organization are mutually achieved.

As we've mentioned previously, this means satisfying not only basic human needs for monetary reward and peer recognition, but also instilling a sense of accomplishment and well-being that comes with making a contribution to the betterment of society as a whole.

Table 11-1 summarizes the attributes necessary for creating and sustaining a culture that supports rapid innovation and learning.

Life-supporting and fulfilling work

A major factor affecting organizational performance is the environment of the knowledge worker. This means providing an ideal environment for fast learning, innovation, and growth.

This also means revisiting and revamping compensation models from traditional hourly or annual pay structures to risk/reward sharing and other performance- and incentive-based models. It also means placing greater emphasis on identifying, tracking, developing, and applying competencies. Compensation systems may vary widely given the nature of the task, project, and mission.

Engaged workforce

Gallop and other polling organizations have made headlines recently regarding their findings that approximately two-thirds of the global workforce is not fully engaged. This has serious negative consequences both over the short and long term. The more knowledge-intensive your enterprise, the more serious the consequences of disengagement and turnover, as critical knowledge walks out the door.

Table 11-1. Growth- and fulfillment-oriented work environments

Focus Areas:	You'll know you're there when:
Life-supporting and fulfilling work	People are passionate about their work, and are driven by a greater goal
	Attracting, retaining, and growing talent are given high priority; compensation systems are performance-based, and take risk vs. reward into account
Engaged workforce	Lessons-learned and best-practice improvements are habitually sought before, during and after a major task or activity
Personal and organizational growth	Each individual knows his/her strengths/weaknesses and has a personal development plan
	Personal knowledge contributes to organizational knowledge and vice versa
Systems mindset	People see the total picture
	Differing perspectives and viewpoints are always taken into account
	Deep learning methods are understood and habitually practiced

The key to reversing this is identifying and strengthening the aspects which drive attraction and retention, particularly those aspects that are engagement-oriented.

In our work, we've found that giving every person an active role in the knowledge transfer process gives a major boost to employee engagement on a sustainable basis. The aspects are twofold: being mentored by one or more people, and being a mentor to one or more people. Both result in personal and organizational growth.

Being mentored provides the ongoing opportunity to learn from the best and more experienced, as well as to grow. Mentoring others provides the satisfaction of making an ongoing contribution, with an eye toward the future, including future generations. Best of all, it reduces wasteful trial-and-error, redundant effort, and repeated mistakes. Definitely a win-win proposition.

Personal and organizational growth

In an age in which we are moving increasingly toward *"business at the speed of thought,"* the growing volume of complexity we have to contend with can slow things down to a crawl. Added complexity pushes back against the demand for faster response. In order to meet this challenge, knowledge must be allowed to flow quickly and easily through the enterprise, increasing in value at each step along the way.

Becoming an enterprise of the future also means enterprise-wide adoption and cultivation of rapid innovation and learning. One way to do this is to design and implement what we call a safe proving ground – an environment which encourages identifying and correcting errors when they are small, long before they grow into costly, repeated mistakes, or worse yet, a catastrophic failure.

The benefits of quickly learning from mistakes and building upon successes should be obvious. Yet this seems to be the most difficult change for organizations to adopt. Overcoming old mindsets and replacing them with new, forward-thinking ones is needed.

Systems-thinking mindset

Dan Holtshouse, Xerox's former Director of Corporate Strategy, understands the need for systems thinking in forward-looking organizations. He writes:

"Business process and organizational changes are sometimes implemented without fully understanding the disruption the changes may have on work patterns and social networks that are the informal bedrock of the workplace. Often unintended consequences produce knowledge bottlenecks and broken processes when initiatives to optimize one asset (say office space costs) cause a sub-optimization to another asset (say the breakup of community work patterns and IT support infrastructure).

What is needed is an integrated, systems thinking approach to the workplace that ensures a more balanced and optimized perspective..."[42]

Many of the problems associated with "not connecting the dots" are a result of drifting away from the underlying reality of the information we receive. We need to expand, not shrink, our peripheral vision as well as our attention span. A good place to start is by looking at our day-to-day problems, opportunities and decisions from more of a systems perspective, rather than only a few narrow segments.

In an information-rich society, the push toward increased reductionism has intensified. From preparing a 30-second sound bite for a news broadcast, to writing a one-page executive decision memorandum, to drawing one of those dreaded "four-part charts," too many of our actions are based upon filtered, summarized information that has lost much of its original context.

Cultivating a systems-thinking mindset involves bringing together many different talents, including:

- ability to work with others both as a team player and leader
- ability to plan and lead projects
- ability to accept responsibility for individual and organizational performance
- passion and ability for creative problem solving
- desire and aptitude for continuous learning
- ability to communicate.

That last one, communication, combined with the skill of facilitation, form the glue that binds workgroups and communities together so members can share knowledge and collaborate effectively.

For many individuals, one or more of the above skills might come naturally. One thing is certain: all of us must be more vigilant in developing, nurturing and growing those skills, and practicing them on a daily basis.

---

[42] Dan Holtshouse, *The Future Workplace*, KMWorld Magazine, June 2006.

Solutions to the complex problems and challenges we are facing cannot be engineered by brute force, as was often the case in the past. Although science and technology are important, success demands engaging brain trusts of individuals with expertise spanning a wide range of disciplines and perspectives. This means combining soft skills with technical expertise. In the enterprise of the future, soft skills are like budgets—surpluses are preferred over deficits.

In sum, rapid innovation and learning should always be a key part of your strategic focus. In fact, systematic attention to knowledge discovery, flow, and retention should be pervasive throughout your enterprise.

Part V

Applying the Framework

Part IV presented a framework which outlined the various building blocks of the enterprise of the future. Here in Part V, we'll examine a series of specific steps you can take to put those building blocks into practice. These steps have been applied in dozens of organizations, large and small, public and private (see Figure V-1).

You can apply each of these steps at a high level, or you can use them to craft strategic initiatives aimed at achieving one or more goals and objectives. Either way, following these four steps will keep you on track in responding to the challenges and opportunities you'll face now and in the years ahead. Here are the steps:

1. Start with Alignment

4. Open the
knowledge floodgates

2. Identify gaps, risks
and opportunities

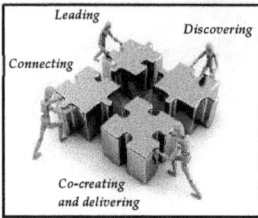

3. Look deep beneath the surface

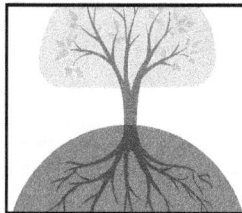

Figure V-1. Four-step process for continuous self-renewal

1. Make sure your strategic goals and objectives, strategy and resources are in alignment (Chapter 12). In other words, clearly define what success looks like, in a measurable way. Then show how your strategic goals and objectives flow down to all levels of your enterprise.

2. Identify major gaps and risks inhibiting or preventing you from achieving your performance goals, along with opportunities (Chapter 13). Most organizational obstacles or barriers come from knowledge not being properly captured, shared, or applied, i.e., *knowledge gaps.* Same goes for identifying and managing *risk.*

At the same time, look for hidden, unexploited capabilities which present *opportunities* for innovation in your products and services, as well as your business model.

3. Look deep beneath the surface for the root causes underlying the gaps, risks, and opportunities (Chapter 14). This step reinforces the need for systems thinking, from re-framing how a problem, risk, or opportunity is expressed, to expanding its context, to identifying root causes and interdependencies.

4. Integrate the various pieces and enable knowledge to flow freely throughout your enterprise (Chapter 15). Making such a transformation happen entails a combination of change initiatives involving people, processes, and technologies.

The benefits of applying this approach are many:

Improved ability to identify critical knowledge gaps, opportunities, and risks, in your organization

In an enterprise of the future, knowledge is the primary form of capital. Just as a financial auditor looks for errors, inconsistencies, and risks regarding an organization's financial capital, you as a social knowledge entrepreneur must take a similar approach to your intellectual assets. By maintaining tight coupling throughout the nine layers we'll outline in the next chapter, you'll be able to more clearly identify knowledge gaps, opportunities and risks impacting your organization's performance.

More efficient and effective use of available resources

Understanding how the key elements in your organization align strategically means you can focus on what's most important, and gain the greatest leverage from the resources you have, including your IT infrastructure. By taking a knowledge-centric view of your organization, you can more clearly identify the decision points in your key processes, where the application of knowledge is vital to success.

In an environment where time is of the essence and resources are constrained, the application of the Pareto Principle, or 80/20 Rule, is more important than ever.

Improved ability to overcome cultural barriers which inhibit execution and resist change

Cultural resistance is difficult to overcome, especially in older organizations. As organizations mature, the original energy behind the founders' vision has long since dissipated, replaced by localized goals and objectives. By reconnecting the work processes with the overall strategy, the workforce recaptures the big picture, and shifts its focus to the achievement of the "greater goal."

Increased performance through better measurement and tracking

When key organizational components are aligned, it becomes easier to measure the contribution of each element to the overall performance of the enterprise. Likewise, the full extent of the impact of interventions on work processes, people, and financial metrics such as cash flow, can be more accurately estimated and verified.

More effective leadership

Leading an agile, global, virtual enterprise requires a new brand of leadership, one which continually reinvents itself. The leader of the future uses every available tool, technique and practice to monitor and anticipate marketplace trends, identify value gaps and opportunities, formulate and execute the right strategy, and adjust accordingly.

Chapter 12

Success Begins and Ends With Alignment[43]

"Alignment of what," you might ask? The answer is *strategy*. Simply stated, strategy: *consists of the guiding principles which define how an enterprise will meet its goals and objectives and achieve its mission.*

Strategy used to be synonymous with "long-term." Strategic plans spanning several decades were not uncommon in the recent past. But as industry clockspeeds began to accelerate, planning horizons dwindled. Now most organizations revisit their strategies annually. Even more frequently, if necessary. Having sufficient agility to change strategic direction can only exist in organizations where

---

[43] This chapter is adapted from a paper by Arthur J. Murray and Kent A. Greenes, *New Leadership Strategies for the Enterprise of the Future*; VINE: The Journal of Information and Knowledge Management Systems, Volume 36, Number 3, 2006, p. 231-237.

communications are clear and timely, and localized goals are closely aligned with strategic goals.

For any enterprise, achieving tight integration across internal and external components is a must. Sustained performance simply isn't possible if there are gaps between the many organizational and infrastructure elements involved. These include business models, information and knowledge flows, human capital, research and development, marketing and sales, customer support, finance and accounting, physical plant and equipment, and intellectual property protection. Indeed, all of the elements of an enterprise, which have typically operated under their own separate processes and systems, need to perform as an integrated whole. This presents a significant challenge in building an enterprise of the future.

When Bill Walsh took over as head coach of the last-place San Francisco 49'ers NFL team in 1979, he didn't instill a winning attitude and the goal of reaching the Super Bowl only in the players and coaches. Everybody, including the receptionists and janitorial staff, had to be on board. And it worked, as they proceeded to win all three of their trips to the Super Bowl.[44]

A leader's greatest challenge is figuring out how to make strategic business decisions without restricting the organization's agility. This means maintaining close coupling up, down and across the organization.

For example, if an organization chooses a product innovation strategy, it needs to first identify the key performance drivers needed to support that strategy. In the case of the *3M Company* for example, rapid concept-to-market cycles are a key performance driver.

Next, the underlying core capabilities needed to achieve that level of performance need to be determined. These core capabilities must be woven tightly together, starting with R&D, and running through

---

[44] Bill Walsh (with Steve Jamison and Craig Walsh), *The Score Takes Care of Itself*, Penguin, 2009.

design, manufacturing, supply chain logistics, marketing, sales and support). Finally, the processes for managing the primary intellectual assets (human, social, structural and organizational) which enable rapid innovation and learning must be thoroughly understood and well-managed. Former Procter & Gamble Chairman and CEO A. G. Lafley and Rotman School of Management Dean Roger L. Martin emphasize the importance not only of alignment but prioritization by *clearly defining success, playing to your strengths* and *only where winning is possible*, and *managing what matters.*[45]

Figure 12-1 illustrates the notion of strategic alignment, in which a strategy is developed top-down, and the execution occurs from the bottom-up. Our experience has shown that the more closely these nine layers are aligned, the better the chance of successfully planning and executing a strategy, and making rapid adjustments as conditions change. A brief description of each layer follows.

Vision. As a leader, the place to start before planning any strategy is the vision for your enterprise. A vision is: *a description of the future you are trying to co-create.* Some examples of vision include:

- A world shaken by radical new technologies, such as:
    - o producing living organisms in the laboratory
    - o non-invasive surgery by nanorobots
    - o dramatically increased lifespan through gene therapy and epigenetics
- "No child left behind"
- Billions of people in developing countries coming online and having access to world markets
- New breakthroughs that will provide cheap, inexhaustible supplies of energy.

---

[45] A. G. Lafley and Roger L. Martin, *Playing to Win: How Strategy Really Works*, Harvard Business Review Press, 2013.

Vision:	*What the world you are trying to co-create will look like*
Mission:	*The impact you will have on the world*
Strategic Goals:	*The ultimate results you want to deliver, and the kind of organization you wish to become*
Strategic Objectives:	*Measurable steps along the way – how you will know how close you are to achieving your strategic goals*
Master Strategy:	*How you will align and focus your resources in order to achieve your strategic goals and objectives*
Performance Drivers:	*The critical factors in your organization that will make the difference between success and failure*
Core Capabilities:	*The ability of your organization to consistently produce a specific result*
Key Process Areas:	*The most efficient and effective aggregation of people and work processes which consistently delivers the desired capability*
Key Enablers:	*Methods, practices and technology infrastructure that enable sustaining high levels of performance*

Human & Social Capital | Organizational & Structural Capital

Figure 12-1. Strategic flow-down from vision to key enablers[46]

---

[46] This framework was adapted from a four-tiered model developed by Accenture (Robert J. Thomas, Peter Cheese, James M. Benton, *Human Capital Development*, Accenture Research Note, November 1, 2003) and expanded to nine levels.

Mission. Having painted the vision, your next step is to *clearly and succinctly define the impact your enterprise will have on the world.* Examples include:

- "Preserving and improving human life."[47]
- "An astronaut walking on Mars by 2030"
- "A cure for cancer within our lifetime"
- The ability to travel anywhere on the globe in four hours or less.

Strategic Goals. Your strategic goals: *capture, in a measurable way, the end results you want to deliver to your clients, and the kind of enterprise you wish to become.* On the external side, a client-centric strategic goal captures the primary benefit clients receive from doing business with you. Internal goals may be more employee- and/or stakeholder-oriented, such as being recognized as one of the *"Top 50 Best Places to Work,"* or making the *"Fast-Growth 100"* list. In either case, they should answer the question, *"Why would someone deal with you instead of your competitor?"*

A strategic goal should be anchored around one or two key elements. It could be size, measure of quality, or strategic positioning in the marketplace, to name a few. Two well-known client-oriented examples are:

- *"Delivered to your door within 30 minutes or it's free"*
- *"When it absolutely, positively has to be there."*

Strategic Objectives. Once you've clearly defined your strategic goals, your strategic objectives: *define how you are going to accomplish your goals.* For example, a strategic goal might be to become a billion-dollar company. In order to get there, depending upon where you're starting from, you may have to increase sales by fifty percent every year for the next seven years.

Strategic objectives and strategy are closely linked. One might drive the other and vice versa. For example, in a product-oriented strategy, a sales target of $1B might require a significant investment in R&D

---

[47] Merck corporate values statement: merck.com/about/mission.html

and marketing. Or the targeted sales growth might be achieved through acquisition.

Strategic objectives are measurable, and should stipulate a time frame. Examples include:

- Revenue growth of 50% per year over the next seven years
- Two new acquisitions per year
- Four new product innovations per year
- Become one of the "top five" in market share within five years.

Master Strategy. Your master strategy: *is a clear, understandable statement of how you will align and focus your resources in order to achieve your strategic goals and objectives.* Master strategies are usually made up of one or more sub-strategies. Some master strategy examples include:

- Market domination through competitive pricing and value chain optimization
- Growth through acquisition
- Pre-eminence through world-class expertise and client education
- Gaining maximum leverage through strategic alliances.

Examples of sub-strategies which support the master strategy include:

- Marketing
  - o Social networking
  - o Saturation advertising
- Sales
  - o Point-of-sale up-selling/cross-selling
  - o Competitive pricing
- Product innovation
  - o Planned product obsolescence in 2-year cycles
- Financial
  - o Leveraged buy-outs
  - o Licensing
- Human capital
  - o 80 hours of specialized training annually

- Customer service
  - A real person answers the phone within two rings, 24/7/365
- Quality
  - Six-sigma, with advancement to seven-sigma.

Performance Drivers. Your organization's performance drivers: *are the primary factors that make the difference between success and failure in achieving your strategic goals and objectives.* For example, if your mission is speed-oriented, such as *"absolutely, positively by 10:00 a.m.,"* or *"delivered in 30 minutes or it's free,"* then your performance drivers should be speed-oriented as well. In this case, the performance demands will be focused on the logistics of preparation, packaging, and delivery.

Likewise, if your primary marketing message is *"if you are dissatisfied for any reason, return the product for a full refund,"* then your major performance drivers will be quality-oriented. A low-price strategy such as Wal-Mart's places huge performance demands on supply-chain systems. Other examples of performance drivers include:

- Consistency
- Efficiency
- Accuracy
- Responsiveness
- Cost control
- Reliability
- Availability
- Asset utilization
- Superior technical support.

Core Capabilities. Your core capabilities are: *the underlying competencies and capacities for producing the results you are promising to deliver.* We divide these into two areas: competency-focused capabilities (*human and social capital*); capacity-oriented capabilities (*organizational and structural capital*).

Examples of human and social capital include:

- Fully certified and accredited support staff
- Fluency in the native languages of our major clients
- Personalized service
- Recognized top experts in the field.

Examples of organizational and structural capital include:
- State-of-the-art testing laboratory
- Mobile showroom
- Electronic Data Interchange (EDI) and other supply-chain infrastructure
- Just-in-time inventory system
- Fully integrated design and production facility
- 24/7/365 call center.

Key Process Areas. We've now "drilled down" far enough to reach the point at which the work is actually performed. We define *work* as the activity that needs to occur in order to produce a specific result. *Work processes* are repeatable models of that activity. The activity can be performed by humans, machines, or both. The goal is to seek the most efficient and effective aggregation of people and work processes which consistently delivers the desired results.

Examples of human and social capital-intensive work processes include:
- Recruitment, hiring and retention
- Sub-contract management
- Relationship management
- Leadership development
- Training and certification.

Examples of organizational and structural capital-intensive work processes include:
- Proposal preparation
- Product life cycle management

- Project management
- Quality management
- Agile development and/or manufacturing.

Key Enablers. Key enablers are: *the methods, practices, and underlying technologies which support the execution of work processes in the most efficient and effective manner possible.* We define *methods* as repeatable formulas, algorithms, rules, techniques, or behaviors underlying a work process. Simply stated, the discovery of a more efficient algorithm, or a more complete set of business rules, could increase the efficiency and effectiveness of a given work process. Examples of methods include:

- Lease vs. buy algorithms
- Source selection methodologies
- Balanced scorecards.

A *practice* is the actual application of a work process within a given organizational context. Examples of practices include:

- Interviewing techniques
- Welcoming/onboarding new employees/associates
- Capturing and sharing lessons learned
- Guidelines for participating in a community of practice.

By technologies we mean tools, techniques and infrastructure that enable efficient and effective performance. Examples of technologies include:

- Platforms
- Data lakes/warehouses
- Virtual/augmented reality
- Mobility
- AI/robotics
- Data analytics.

Improving alignment by unclogging the knowledge pipeline[48]

By now it should be clear that in order to achieve high-speed innovation and learning, knowledge needs to flow unimpeded throughout the enterprise. The growing volume of information we have to contend with can slow things down to a crawl. Added complexity pushes back against the demand for faster response. In order to meet this challenge, knowledge must be allowed to flow quickly and easily throughout the enterprise, increasing in value at each step along the way.

All too often, the knowledge pipeline becomes clogged. The natural tendency for organizations to break up into silos is a commonly accepted reason for impeded knowledge flows. However, if we look a little deeper we find that even if organizational barriers are removed, knowledge still doesn't flow as freely as we would like. This is due to a condition we call *misalignment*.

Misalignment is: *the condition whereby effective and timely communication is impeded. Communication,* simply stated, is: *the process by which actionable information is transmitted by one agent and received by another.* Note that we use the word *agent* to account for humans, organizations and machines, since many activities leading up to critical decisions are performed by individuals, technologies, or collections of both.

Misalignment often shows up when departments such as contracting, finance, HR, marketing and IT all need to be involved in an activity such as a joint problem-solving session. A large part of what makes managing knowledge flows so difficult comes from the many different perspectives among the agents which are communicating.

Consider, for example, the need for eliciting inputs for developing and marketing a new product from subject matter experts, software developers, users, and procurement officers. These inputs will be viewed by some in terms of functional capability, by others in terms of

---

[48] Adapted from Brian Newman and Art Murray, *Unclogging the Knowledge Pipeline*, KMWorld Magazine, Nov/Dec, 2010.

system design features and parameters, and by others in terms of costs, performance results, or outcomes. A supposedly simple notion of requirements ends up having many different meanings, depending upon the perspective of each of the parties involved. Unfortunately, such differences may not be discovered until after-the-fact, when a so-called "solution" is delivered only to be sent back to the drawing board at significant additional cost.

Differences in the knowledge, skills and abilities of people and their systems (especially databases) further contribute to misalignment. A familiar example of this occurs when experts attempt to transfer their knowledge to novices.

This condition is often exacerbated when organizations attempt to force communications into a rigid template. Valuable context is lost by being squeezed through the narrow aperture of a single perspective.

An enterprise of the future focuses on alignment from the get-go: from planning to execution, from forming a team to developing requirements, and for all related problem-solving and decision-making activity. This especially applies when forming teams. Don't leave essential people out because they might not fit in. At the same time, you can't drop a detail-oriented accountant or engineer into a room with a bunch of impatient sales-driven marketing execs and expect a smooth transfer of knowledge to occur. A facilitator needs to be added to the mix in order to help close the semantic divide.

Make sure your team is facilitated by someone with the necessary soft skills to keep the conversation open and honest, with everyone contributing. This is where the "soft skills" of facilitation come into play. Facilitators pull the subject matter experts out of their silos, helping to build and grow a more unified brain trust. The biggest challenge is avoiding the temptation of trying to find the least common denominator, resulting in a subpar outcome.

Finally, misalignment directly translates into increased risk exposure. Not paying close attention to alignment means unnecessarily exposing your enterprise to adverse cost, schedule, and performance impacts.

The old project management-oriented mindset of critical path alignment focuses only on time. By shifting your viewpoint to critical alignment of knowledge flows, you can better manage not only time, but cost and performance as well.

Chapter 13

Identifying Gaps, Risks and Opportunities

You've defined what you mean by success. You've painted a vision of the future, the impact you'll co-create, and a strategy for getting there. You've identified and aligned the resources you have at your disposal including people, processes and technologies (human and social capital, and organizational and structural capital).

If it were only that simple. By their very nature, strategic goals and objectives should extend beyond where you are today. If there weren't any barriers, obstacles or risks along the way, they wouldn't be worth pursuing.

In this next step, we'll show you how to: take a closer look at the resources you already have; see what's missing; fill in the gaps. In all likelihood you'll discover hidden, unexploited capabilities that will not only help you close the gaps and reduce risk, but also spawn new, unforeseen opportunities.

When looking at barriers and obstacles it pays to find out why they exist in the first place. For example, one barrier that seems to come up quite often is "We don't have enough funding." If you ask, "Why not?" you might hear something like, "well, 'so-and-so' always gets funded, leaving little or nothing for us." If you ask, "Why is that?" you might hear, because the Board gives them whatever they ask for." "And why is that?" "Because they know how to work the system."

Aha! Finally, after asking *why, why, why* enough times, you see that one little word, as in: "They *know* how to work the system." In other words, they have the knowledge and you don't. You've just identified a *knowledge gap*.

You may even have the knowledge, but you're just not applying it correctly. Either way, what appears on the surface to be a political obstacle to obtaining funding is really a knowledge gap.

Such gaps are a major source of inefficiency in an organization. We define knowledge gaps as *essential knowledge that's missing, unavailable, or difficult to obtain or apply.*

According to a study by Cotrill Research, knowledge workers spend 15% to 30% or more of their time looking for information.[49] In many instances, the knowledge exists but is never found because people give up looking.

On the opportunity side, performing a knowledge asset inventory can reveal hidden knowledge assets, and identify new sources of revenue. Since performing an audit of its own intellectual property, Texas Instruments has realized over $100B in revenue from licensing,

---

[49] Cotrill Research, *Various Survey Statistics: Workers Spend Too Much Time Searching For Information*, Nov 8, 2013.

royalties, and patent infringements. IBM realizes approximately $2B annually from its IP portfolio. Rockwell, Dow Chemical, and Procter & Gamble have implemented similar programs.[50]

This presents another problem. With all that knowledge swimming around inside an organization, how do you know which knowledge is valuable and which isn't? For that, you simply go back to the nine-layer flow-down chart in Figure 12-1.

But there's an easier way, if you're in a pinch. At least it's a way to get started.

First of all, it helps to define what we mean by knowledge. Simply stated, *knowledge is the capacity to take effective action in varied and uncertain situations.*[51] A key part of the capacity to take effective action includes *observing* and *deciding* which action to take.

Because knowledge covers such a wide spectrum, it pays to focus only on highly specialized knowledge that's critical to your organization's success. It's particularly important if such knowledge is at risk of being lost or compromised. This includes critical knowledge that essentially disappears every time a key associate walks out the door at the end of the work day. And it leaves for good when that person decides to quit or retire. This creates a serious risk for any organization.

It even gets more difficult in situations where most of the critical knowledge is of the tacit variety. Tacit knowledge is: *knowledge that is so deeply internalized you would have difficulty explaining it to someone or putting it into writing.* As opposed to explicit knowledge, such as a set of clearly defined rules (*"if X happens, then do Y"*), tacit knowledge is usually governed by deep intuition. You may have heard someone say, "I can't tell you what it looks like, but I'll know it when I see it." That's usually an indicator of deep tacit knowledge at work.

---

[50] Dickstein Shapiro Morin & Oshinsky LLP, *Intellectual Property Primer*, Association of Corporate Counsel, May 2005, p. 28.
[51] A. Bennet & D. Bennet, *Organizational Survival in the New World: The Intelligent Complex Adaptive System*, Elsevier, 2004.

You can get started down the path of critical knowledge capture and transfer by asking your key people the following:

"What is the single, most important thing you do in your job that nobody else really knows or understands – that if for some reason you didn't show up for work for a certain period of time, a huge gap would form and our ability to succeed in our mission would be seriously impacted?"

As we've mentioned earlier, don't forget the *why* and the *how*. In other words, why that particular piece of knowledge is critical, how the experts do what they do, and why they do it that way. It's amazing how many leaders in organizations can't answer those simple questions.

The answers are always there. It just takes work to draw them out. Sometimes a lot of work. This is where the elements of *change* and *trust* come into play, which we'll discuss later in Part VI.

Chapter 14

Looking Deep Beneath the Surface

We can view our world from two directions. One is from the outside looking in. This is where most of the attention is currently focused. It's been greatly amplified in recent decades by the ability to computationally analyze massive volumes of structured and unstructured data.

Yet even with the most powerful sensors and processors, including the forthcoming leaps in quantum computing (see Chapter 6, Opportunity #2), we still can't account for all possible combinations and permutations. This is the inherent limitation of big data analytics.

Another problem with this approach is the *fallacy of induction*. "You should lower your cholesterol." "No, wait – you should raise your good cholesterol and lower your bad cholesterol." "No, wait – it's your high triglycerides that are killing you." And so on.

133

One way to manage this is to treat all rules as what Karl Popper calls *falsifiable.*[52] In other words, a generally accepted set of rules holds true until such time as those rules are proven false. At which point they are modified and updated.

Viewing the world from a deep structure level

The other direction from which you can view the world is identifying the basic elements and rules of aggregation underlying a particular area of investigation, and working your way up. Of course, the basic elements and rules of aggregation need to be discovered. That's not easy, especially given limitations such as the fallacy of induction.

Nevertheless, assembling a set of basic elements and associated rules of aggregation provide a more stable basis for investigation, discovery, and decision-making. We refer to this as *deep structure* (recall Opportunity #7 in Chapter 6).

The notions of time variance and time invariance come into play as well. Hint: the deeper you go, the longer the time constants become, as the underlying structure moves from time-variant to time-invariant.

In linguistics, for example, the basic elements (phonemes) are essentially time-invariant. Rules of grammar are time-variant, but their time constants are measured in durations of centuries or longer, for example, current English grammar versus Chaucerian grammar. Syntactical aggregations change more frequently, sometimes over a period of only a few decades.

Root sounds, when combined in ways that are syntactically and semantically correct, make sense. Other combinations which violate the rules of syntax and grammar make no sense. Unless of course, the combination represents a new type of expression, in which case the rules of syntax and grammar are modified.

---

[52] Karl R. Popper, *Objective Knowledge: An Evolutionary Approach* (revised edition), Oxford University Press, 1979, p. 13-17.

We've mentioned repeatedly that the world is growing more complex at an ever-faster rate. Given that's true, and the world continues along the course of scientific reductionism as a means of managing the ever-expanding volume of observable data, critical contextual factors will inevitably be overlooked. As a result, we continue to repeat mistakes and "re-invent the wheel," while our experience of "drowning in information while being starved for knowledge" intensifies.

This is evidenced in many organizations by the constant pressure to encapsulate knowledge into bite-sized, memorable "nuggets." For example, a top portfolio manager in the financial sector might give an apprentice a set of catchy phrases like: "When volatility is high, we buy; when volatility is low, we go...now get to work!"

The apprentice applies the rules and does rather well. That is, until the rules no longer work. Or until external conditions change so wildly and rapidly it's almost impossible to decide which course of action to take. This happens because the underlying sense that created the rules is missing.

The expert, now long gone, possessed something innate that didn't get imparted to the novice—the capacity to deal with novelty. The expert knows when the rules work and when to break them. But ask that same expert to explain how to tell the difference, and the response usually goes something like: "I really don't know why I know, or how I know ... I just know."

In the crunch for time, experts are often forced to give "CliffsNotes" versions of what they know. Such oversimplification fails to consider the stratified deep structure involved in human sense making. Breaking the shallow learning barrier means transferring not only the rules but also the underlying processes generating the rules. That can only occur through repetitive cycles of observation, self-directed inquiry, and self-discovery. The field of neuropsychology gives us a better understanding of how to tap into those processes.[53]

---

[53] Karl Pribram, *The Deep and Surface Structure of Memory and Conscious Learning: Toward*

Peter Senge's *system archetypes* are another good example of deep structure. Some of his more notable archetypes include: delayed feedback loops; limits to growth; "shifting the burden;" goal erosion; "tragedy of the commons."[54]

We've only given you a tiny glimpse into the world of deep structure. In the era of big data, with innumerable zettabytes swirling around, it's easy to lose sight of the fact that there are time-invariant structures at the heart of it all.

Here are a few steps you can take to help keep things in perspective:

<u>1. Expand your knowledge horizons and learn to see deep structure everywhere</u>. Apply this thought process to anything in need of greater clarity: business intelligence; intellectual property; marketing; public relations; strategy; workflow; policies and procedures; knowledge sharing and transfer.

Come up with your own list of semantic primes. Which base emotions or values are driving your enterprise? A sense of fulfillment? Destroying the competition? A sense of sharing or stewardship? How well are they reflected in your narrative?

Go beyond just looking at words themselves, which are purely surface-level phenomena. Instead, pay close attention to their basic "atomic" structure and valences. Does the vocabulary used in your social discourse attract or repel? Does it tend to be soft or percussive? Open or closed? Which leads us to...

<u>2. Spot trends sooner by engaging in the social discourse within and outside your organization</u>. Start building *ontologies* and putting them to use. Determine what rules of semantic aggregation are in play.

With practice, intent will become more transparent with less chance for deception. You'll be able to better identify and correct false or negative memes that have been adversely impacting not only public

---

a 21st Century Model, op.cit.
[54] Peter M. Senge, *The Fifth Discipline*, Doubleday/Currency, 1990.

perception about you and your enterprise, but also your own self-image.

3. Stop dumbing down and reverse the semantic loss that comes with it. That doesn't mean going back to the jargon-heavy styles that everyone rebelled against and that brought us to where we are today. But you should ignore the prevailing wisdom, which is to communicate at no higher than a seventh- or eighth-grade level. Rather, focus on keeping things simple *and* deep, as opposed to simple and shallow.

Identify the minimal set of semantic primes you need to deliver as clear and unambiguous a message as possible. Remember, the use of surface-level or shallow semantics quickly breaks down in complex, rapidly changing situations. Deep structure allows you to navigate the complexity without being overwhelmed.

Make these three steps a regular habit. Too many decisions with disastrous consequences are made based on knee-jerk reactions that come from looking only at what appears on the surface. One video clip. A single tweet. A comment taken out of context.

There is surface structure and deep structure everywhere. In geopolitics. Global trade and finance. Climate and the environment. The human mind and body, both individual and societal.

An enterprise of the future needs to achieve a balance between tactics and strategy. You do that by keeping a close eye on surface phenomena (tactics) while peeling away the onion layers to reveal the underlying deep structure (strategy).

Probing deep structure exposes hidden interdependencies and possible unintended consequences of a proposed course of action. Very few organizations do this on a regular basis, if at all. Just make sure you're not one of them.

Chapter 15

Opening the Knowledge Floodgates

You've aligned strategy with available resources. You've identified critical knowledge gaps, risks and opportunities, and viewed them from a deep structure level. All that remains is putting together an executable plan for closing the gaps, mitigating the risks, and seizing the opportunities.

At this point the most important thing to remember is not to try and do everything all at once. Whether you're building an enterprise of the future from scratch as a startup, or transforming an existing enterprise, it's vitally important to balance and prioritize.

One way to do this is through a program of focused strategic initiatives aimed at creating the capacity for rapid innovation and learning in a selected area. Preferably an area in which you can achieve the greatest impact with the least amount of effort. Ideally, your plan should focus on enabling and enhancing critical knowledge flows internally and externally across your enterprise.

Here are seven action steps you can take in order to properly craft that set of strategic initiatives:

<u>Step 1</u>. List the key change drivers (internal and external) impacting your ability to succeed (both positively and negatively).

<u>Step 2</u>. In the face of these change drivers, determine *what* needs to change in your enterprise in order to address the gaps, risks and opportunities you've identified. Be sure to include each of the four areas of *leading, connecting, co-creating* and *discovering*. This will help reveal the *who* and the *where*.

<u>Step 3</u>. Remember to not only identify *who* and *what* needs to change and *where*, but *why* those changes need to be made. Most importantly, make sure you clearly determine what will happen if you do *not* make the needed changes.

Having identified the *what, who, where*, and *why*, you can now address the *how*.

<u>Step 4</u>. Determine exactly how you will make the needed changes happen at a systemic, deep structure level, as opposed to piecemeal, "point solutions." In almost all cases in which systemic "root causes" are addressed, impediments to the flow of knowledge will enter into the discussion. In fact, when discussing knowledge flows, it pays to look at every point in the *knowledge life cycle*, which consists of the three steps of *capture, share*, and *apply* (see Figure 15-1).

If the root causes of the gaps, risks and opportunities involve a lack of knowledge, then it's likely a knowledge *capture* issue. Knowledge capture means being able to identify and access the knowledge needed to succeed, in ways that it can be adapted, refined, and re-used.

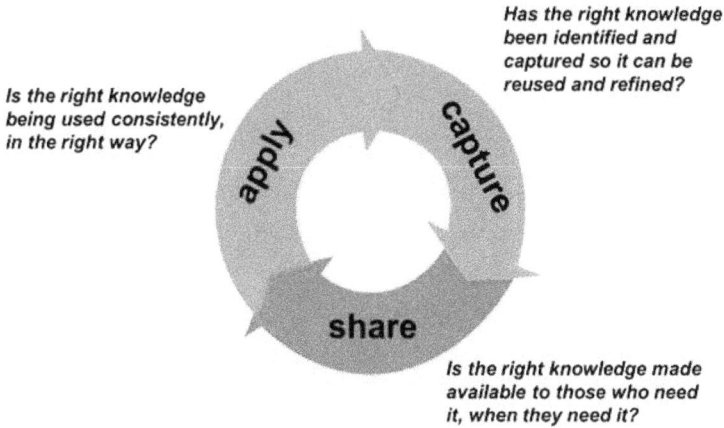

Figure 15-1. The knowledge life cycle

Sometimes the right knowledge exists, but it isn't *shared* due to cultural or other barriers. Having the right knowledge isn't enough. You need to make sure it's freely available to those who need it, when they need it.

But capturing and sharing knowledge still doesn't go far enough. All of the knowledge in the world is useless if it's *misapplied*. Your organization's critical knowledge must be used consistently in ways that produce the desired outcomes as frequently as possible.

As you build your strategic change initiatives, you should be working your way down the strategic alignment pyramid (shown earlier in Figure 12-1). This means carefully evaluating and assigning the right people (human and social capital), processes and technologies (organizational and structural capital).

<u>Step 5</u>. Next, come up with a realistic timeframe for making the changes happen, i.e., the *when*.

<u>Step 6</u>. This leads to establishing performance metrics such as KPIs (key performance indicators) which you'll need in order to answer the critical question: *"How will we know if all of this is working?"*

<u>Step 7</u>. Be sure to thoroughly document the previous six steps for future reference. This helps you to avoid repeating mistakes and duplicating effort. An *option outline* is an excellent way to capture the thought process that went into the key decisions made along the way.[55]

Finally, as a leader, make sure the words *"That'll never work here"* are never uttered. Instead, instill a culture in which everyone asks, *"How can we make this work?"*

---

[55] John Lewis, *The Explanation Age* (3rd edition), *op.cit.*, p. 51-64.

Part VI

Making Transformation Happen

You've completed the planning part. Now comes the execution. The doing.

The world is in a continual state of flux. That's why the type of enterprise we've envisioned demands a continuous cycle of renewal. In fact, many of your assumptions are likely to be rendered at least partially invalid right from the get-go.

With that in mind, here are some additional approaches, mindsets and practices you can use along the way to help keep you on course when the course keeps changing. One, known as Theory of Change, puts some structure around the turbulence associated with change. It does this by instilling a mindset of focusing on *outcomes* as opposed to the normal tendency to focus on *activities*. And in a world fraught with risk, we also need to discuss ways to watch out for and avoid the many pitfalls we're likely to encounter, both foreseen and unforeseen.

We'll add a subtle reminder that it isn't always about technology. The human element is of equal or even greater importance. We'll address three key elements that are found wanting in today's extremely competitive environment: ethics, values and trust. Finally, we look at one pioneering enterprise of the future that has managed to stitch together many of the pieces we've been talking about.

Chapter 16

Applying Theory of Change[56]

In order to build and sustain an enterprise of the future, you need a robust, adaptable planning process. One of the traps to avoid when formulating a plan is the tendency to focus on activities. Most plans start with what needs to be done today (what you know) and work towards a future goal (what you don't know). The problem with that approach is as soon as your plan goes into effect, many of the assumptions on which it was based will have already changed.

This calls for a planning framework that's stable with regard to the envisioned end state, yet agile enough to adjust along the way. That's where *Theory of Change* comes in.

ActKnowledge defines Theory of Change as: "*a rigorous yet participatory process whereby groups and stakeholders in a planning process articulate their long-term goals and identify the conditions they believe have to unfold for those goals to*

---

[56] Adapted from Art Murray and Greg Larsen, *A Framework for Change*, KMWorld Magazine, February, 2017.

be met."[57]   In other words, the focus is placed on achieving specific *outcomes* and defining the programs or initiatives (i.e., interventions) needed to achieve those outcomes, along with measurable indicators of progress.   This results in a *causal* framework that reveals, as ActKnowledge puts it, the *"complex web of activity required to bring about change."*[58]

We define outcomes as: *desired or necessary, plausibly achievable conditions.* The pathway to an outcome consists of the many pre-conditions that contribute to it.   Pathways are built using a technique known as *backwards mapping.*   Instead of starting from where you are today and moving forward in incremental steps, you mentally "leap ahead" to the envisioned end state and work back to the present.

Theory of Change has been used successfully by a wide variety of organizations, including the Annie E. Casey Foundation,[59] the Overseas Development Institute (ODI) and The Hunger Project, to name a few.   For additional details, check out theoryofchange.org, which also has a tool you can download for building visual representations of the backwards-mapping pathways, known as *outcome maps.*[60]

In a nutshell, here are the five steps:

Step 1. Based on observed and anticipated trends in technology, society, politics, economics and other key areas, define the future state of your competitive environment in terms of threats, challenges and opportunities.   Assign a timeframe for when you expect that future state to fully materialize.

---

[57] Taplin, D. H., & Clark, H. *Theory of Change Basics: A Primer on Theory of Change.* ActKnowledge. March 2012, p. 1.
[58] *ibid.*
[59] Organizational Research Services, *Theory of Change: A Practical Tool For Action, Results and Learning,* Annie E. Casey Foundation, 2004.
[60] For an example of a completed outcome map, visit the Hunger Project's site at thp.org/our-work/measuring-our-work/theory-change

<u>Step 2</u>. For the same timeframe, define the desired future state of your enterprise in a way that addresses the competitive environment envisioned in Step 1.

<u>Step 3</u>. Establish a timeline consisting of three phases: long-term, intermediate-term, and short-term. The length of each phase will vary depending upon your industry's clockspeed (recall Chapter 2). For each phase, define the outcomes needed to advance toward the desired future end state.

Remember to always start at the end and work back, rather than vice versa. Doing this helps you avoid wasting precious time and resources responding to short-term "pop-up" requirements that have little to do with getting to your desired end state.

<u>Step 4</u>. Organize the outcomes into relevant strategic categories. These may include policies, business models, processes, technologies, standards, and the like. Extend each category of outcomes across the three time phases.

<u>Step 5</u>. Establish the metrics you'll use to track progress toward achieving the outcomes. In an environment characterized by rapidly accelerating changes in speed and complexity, organizational performance depends in large part upon the capacity to quickly access information and take effective action. This is best represented by using the *five V's* of volume, veracity, value, variety and velocity.

When properly formulated, these and other metrics will provide a basis to discern where current operations, activities or capabilities will fall short or put at risk the attainment of a future state. They also enable you to evaluate the progress of stakeholders. As such they need to be assessed at multiple points along the pathways from one condition (outcome) to another and ultimately to the final outcome, so that adjustments can be made as needed along the way.

An illustrative example

A current topic of discussion is the growing trend toward automation of a wide range of functions and tasks traditionally performed by humans. From cashiers to construction workers to lawyers, accountants and medical doctors, large segments of the workforce are in danger of being displaced.

Let's say you're in the retail industry. You've already been struggling with the move toward online shopping. To make matters worse, you've seen the entry into the market of *AmazonGo*. Their newly designed "bricks and mortar" store has no cashiers and no checkout counters. All items are electronically tracked and charged to your account via your smart phone as soon as you place them into your shopping cart. Given that backdrop, here's how you might apply the five steps of Theory of Change to your strategic planning process.

Step 1. In 5 to 7 years (or sooner), key disruptions will likely include drone and autonomous vehicle delivery systems, blockchain payment ledgers, Internet of Things (IoT) and models accurately predicting what customers will need before they even realize it.

Step 2. Taking advantage of some of the above disruptive technologies, your future state might be characterized by near-instantaneous response to social discourse (both positive and negative) and exploitation of the "maker" economy by allowing products to be manufactured as close to the customer as possible using 3-D printing.

Step 3. Long-term outcomes might include optimized pricing models that grow market share in an economic environment of stagnant wages and large segments of an aging population living on fixed incomes (business models).

Intermediate-term outcomes might include a tightly integrated supply chain with highly automated packing and shipping enabled by intelligent robots and drones (processes, technologies and standards) and community outreach programs to help retrain displaced workers (policies, processes).

Short-term outcomes might include establishing suitable partnerships and/or acquisitions to aid in competitive positioning and maintaining market leadership.

Step 4. Major outcome categories include policies, processes, technology, and standards. Policies need to address current and even possible future situations, along with legal, ethical, and liability concerns. Processes and technology together must provide clear and consistent ways of employing increased automation and AI, especially in areas such as business intelligence, planning, and decision-making. Finally, standards ensure that the many different components, particularly brought about by the Internet of Things, actually talk to each other.

Step 5. All of the envisioned outcomes exemplify the need for information with high levels of all five Vs. For example, the short-term outcome to establish suitable partnerships and/or acquisitions will require more timely and effective due diligence.

Actions to take

Begin incorporating Theory of Change across your enterprise. Be sure to evangelize and involve as many key stakeholders as possible. Then brainstorm steps 1 and 2. At the very least, it will get you started down the path of aligning your current efforts with your intermediate and long-term goals.

Start formulating specific initiatives that will focus your resources by systematically moving toward the desired future state, rather than waiting for things to happen and reacting to them. Be sure to incorporate the five Vs and other change drivers into your key performance indicators (KPIs). The more information-intensive your enterprise, the more closely you'll need to track them.

Finally, make this an annual process, even semi-annual, depending upon the speed of change in your market. In a world that appears to be spinning out of control, applying Theory of Change will help direct your efforts in ways that will have the greatest positive impact. Best of all, you'll enjoy the benefits of having a greater hand in co-creating the future, rather than continually reacting to it.

Chapter 17

Managing Risk[61]

It's important to remember that we might not even make it to the point of eight billion minds and 100 billion devices if everything comes crashing down. As systems of systems, even entire civilizations, grow increasingly complex they consume ever-increasing amounts of energy. If allowed to grow unchecked, such systems will collapse under their own weight.

We should certainly make every effort to maintain a positive outlook. After all, we're co-creating our own shared future state. We must do our utmost to envision and achieve the very best poss3ible outcomes.

---

[61] Adapted from Art Murray, *Assessing and Mitigating Risk*, KMWorld Magazine, November/December, 2016.

At the same time, it's important to keep in mind that things don't always go as planned. There are bumps, even serious setbacks along the way. That's why no matter where you are in your strategic planning cycle, you should always keep an eye on what risks you may encounter and how best to avoid, mitigate or, if necessary, respond to them.

A brave new world (even a boring old one) always carries the risk of unforeseen events – both breakthroughs and catastrophes. We, our enterprises, and our societies need to be able to, as best we can, plan for and respond to such events.

A sound risk management strategy includes an assessment of your most critical assets. Those strategic assets usually consist of your people, infrastructure and customers. That means looking at risk from both the physical and human side of things. Not separately, but as an integrated whole.

In that regard, it pays to be on guard for three categories of events in particular. We playfully refer to them as: things that go *bang*, things that go *dark*, and things that go *boing*.

Things that go bang

While not exactly widespread, recent events have exposed the physical vulnerability of many organizations, including the possibility of personal injury or loss of life, brought about by individuals and organizations bent on destruction.

If you work for a government agency or large enterprise, especially where physical security is a priority, your personal safety is better than it would be in many other situations. When destructive forces are planning their next move, they usually avoid heavily fortified structures and instead look for what are called "soft targets."

But if your organization doesn't have the budget for concrete and steel barriers, security guards, strong access/egress controls and the like, take heart. A little knowledge goes a long way.

For example, the Red Cross has been accumulating and making available a large, multilingual knowledge library on prevention and response to all types of disasters, including terrorism and civil unrest (redcross.org/prepare/disaster-safety-library). It includes mobile apps and a wide assortment of training modules for you and your fellow employees.

Browsing through their knowledge base, you'll see that physical safety doesn't always involve human threats. Recent storms, earthquakes and even health hazards such as the Zika, Ebola, and other viruses have shown that nature can be just as or even more dangerous.

As a leader of an enterprise of the future, you fully understand and appreciate the value of human capital. You invest heavily in training, mentoring, career management and the like. But if you aren't already doing so, you also need to start paying attention to the physical well-being and protection of your workforce.

Things that go dark

In addition to physical security you need to guard against cyberattack and systems failures in general. Many don't realize just how tightly coupled cyber and physical systems have become. The boundaries between the two are now at the point of being nearly indistinguishable.

Think about how "tethered" you are to everything: the power grid, communications and transportation networks, fuel/charging stations, food and medical supplies, indoor environmental systems. A growing part of daily activities that take place in your home, neighborhood, workplace, exercise room are all tied to what's now being called the cyber-physical infrastructure. And the growing number of interconnections and interdependencies are creating serious risks and vulnerabilities.

That means your "need to know what you know" has greatly expanded beyond human capital to knowing: 1) what "smart" components are part of your critical infrastructure, 2) how they are all interconnected, and 3) how much, if any, human control remains. That third part can be a real eye-opener, especially as the Internet of Things (IoT) continues its rapid expansion. As you build that extended knowledge asset inventory, pay particular attention to those critical interconnections that, if taken out, could make your entire operation go dark.

Again, vast storehouses of knowledge are available to draw from. *InfraGard* has resources spanning 16 critical infrastructure areas.[62] The U.S. National Institute of Standards and Technology (NIST) Engineering Laboratory has an entire site devoted to cyber-physical systems, along with a definitive *Community Resilience Planning Guide*.[63] Those are just a few of the many knowledge resources available to help strengthen your resilience across a full spectrum of risks.

Things that go boing

As we've discussed earlier in Chapter 5, Challenge #2, the technical term for "*things that go boing*" is *technology-driven social amplification*. This is when a single "tweet" or video clip rapidly spreads, fueling emotions which can quickly amplify, possibly leading to anything ranging from a boycott of your products to a total breakdown of social cohesion.

This particular risk category can be the most problematic because despite the improved capability of modeling these types of social phenomena, the outcomes can still be highly unpredictable.[64] If you haven't already done so, start thinking about what policies, plans and processes you need to have in place to stay on top of the constantly changing social discourse in all areas affecting your enterprise.

There are numerous other risks you need to be mindful of, such as political, legal and regulatory, economic, supply chain and perhaps most important of all, disruptive innovation. Many of those risks are

---

[62] infragard.org/
[63] nist.gov/el/cyber-physical-systems
[64] R. E. Kasperson, et al., *The Social Amplification of Risk: A Conceptual Framework, op cit.*

interconnected and interdependent. One can easily lead to another and then another, in cascading fashion.

Advances in technology can be both constructive and destructive, so be sure to use them to your advantage. For example, you can use an assortment of tools such as big data analytics, link analysis, and semantic analysis to discover hidden trends and patterns that can help you better prepare for and respond to emerging threats as well as opportunities, both internal and external.

Remember, you can be the one creating the disruptive innovation in your industry, rather than reacting to somebody else's. Finally, make sure that access to your critical data, as well as to your key subject matter experts and decision makers, doesn't have to pass through a single "choke point."

It may be unpleasant to think about all the terrible things that can happen. But to do nothing exposes you, your organization and your loved ones to unnecessary risk.

Remain vigilant, armed with the right knowledge. So no matter what happens along the way, you'll be able to continue blazing a trail to a brighter future.

Chapter 18

Enough Technology Already, What About Us Humans?

In Chapter 6, Opportunities #5 and #6, we discussed emerging technologies and their potential for increasing longevity. What's often overlooked is the need for improvement in how we currently practice medicine.

In the medical field, two parameters are vitally important: speed and accuracy. On the speed side, we need to overcome the glacial pace at which the results of medical research work their way into clinical practice (recall Challenge #5 in Chapter 5). A major reason for this is misalignment across various lexicons, skill and experience levels, age groups, geographic regions, ethnicities and cultures, to name a few.

On the accuracy side, medical errors remain a stubborn obstacle, much for the same reasons. While we've been making excellent progress in the area of evidence-based medical research, the application of the results of that research is often inconsistent. Most of the knowledge flows in one direction, with little feedback from the field. If somebody in practice discovers a more effective way of implementing research results under certain conditions, that knowledge usually remains localized, only to be "rediscovered" in other places through needless trial and error.[65] This presents a tremendous opportunity.

Excellent progress has been made toward building a high-assurance infrastructure for electronic medical records. Simply eliminating the redundancy and errors associated with having those records scattered and fragmented across incompatible systems is a giant step toward increased efficiency and improved accuracy.

The next challenge is delivering expert knowledge along with patient data directly to the point of decision, which is where many of the errors causing injury and death occur. Sometimes it may be a single decision, with a person's life hanging in the balance. Or, as is often the case, it's a series of small, seemingly minor decisions which taken together can mean the difference between death or recovery.

Connecting apparently unrelated dots is a must if we are to maintain a grip on our increasingly complex healthcare system. Medical practitioners, insurers, administrators, equipment manufacturers, operators and technicians, patients, families and researchers all need to be on the same page. That means not only connecting the dots, but also getting knowledge to flow among those dots quickly and easily, making sure nothing gets lost in translation.

Imagine how much the world would benefit by removing the guesswork that accompanies medical practice. For example, by mapping the interdependencies among various known elements such as a patient's family medical history, food intolerances, metabolism, blood chemistry, cultural background, even stress and previous

---

[65] Dr. Richard Van West-Charles and Dr. Arthur J. Murray, *Formulating KM Strategies at the Local Level: A New Approach to Knowledge Sharing in Large Public Health Organizations*, Knowledge Management in Public Health, Jay Liebowitz, Richard A. Schieber, and Joanne Andreadis, eds., CRC Press, 2010.

trauma, the chances of success are greatly increased. If the potential cost of all this seems daunting, consider that currently in the United States alone more than $300 billion per year is wasted through incorrect treatments and misdiagnoses.[66]

Expanding our view further, we find a myriad of different types of people and organizations, each looking after their own interests. The human and organizational dots that need connecting include primary care physicians, surgeons, oncologists and other specialists, nurse practitioners, pharmacists, dieticians, psychiatrists and psychologists, exercise/conditioning coaches, family members, financial planners, insurers, government auditors, attorneys and more. Each group speaks a different language and views the world of medicine from a different perspective.

For example, medical doctors receive a steady stream of published research that is often indecipherable (even for them) and difficult to apply in daily practice, for many different reasons. Even in cases in which the research is applied, crossing organizational boundaries and feeding observations from the field back to the research community can be daunting. While all of those players don't necessarily need to speak the same language (although Latin still seems to be hanging on for dear life), they do need to be on the same page.

We need to find ways in which we can work with all the players in the medical community to help make the transformation to a new, patient-centered system. This will have the net effect of pushing knowledge and its application out to the patient in a helpful, non-judgmental way. Making the shift toward a patient-centered experience for education and behavioral reinforcement for healthy living should be the end vision. A shrinking pool of medical doctors relative to population growth makes this transformation even more urgent.

---

[66] U.S. Department of Health and Human Services, op cit.

Tapping an immense pool of knowledge from within

Surprisingly, the next leap in human evolution may actually be viewed as a step backward. That's because it's been around for as long as humans have inhabited the earth. Maybe even longer. It's a network more massive than the fictional *Skynet*, with trillions of nodes and innumerable connections. And it's not something "out there." This recently discovered organ exists inside each and every one of us.

At four pounds, the human microbiome displaces the liver as the heaviest organ in the body. An ecosystem within an ecosystem, the microbiome is a complex matrix of microbes including bacteria, yeast, fungi, viruses and even parasites. It has its own DNA library, with approximately eight million genes. It produces 32 known neurotransmitters, including 50 percent of the dopamine and 90 percent of the serotonin present in the body.

The human microbiome is as close to an operating system as anything else in the body. It regulates the processing of nutrients, guards against toxins, and regulates backup power (in the form of fat). It supports cognitive functions such as memory storage and retrieval, making sense of sensory inputs, decision-making, and much more.

This isn't some new age idea or natural health fad. Hundreds of peer-reviewed papers have been published, with more than $170 million invested in research to date.[67]

What it all means

These discoveries have the potential for creating major disruption in several areas. One is in the rapidly changing field of nutrition. Nutrition is a foundational building block of human intelligence. This is partially borne out in studies that show abnormally low IQ levels prevalent among people in poorer countries.

---

[67] You can get a glimpse into this exciting and rapidly expanding world at commonfund.nih.gov/hmp.

Recent studies have shown that malnutrition is pervasive in developed countries as well, but for different reasons. It results primarily from the inability of the body to properly absorb the nutrients it takes in. The long-term neglect and degradation of the microbiome makes it harder to absorb proteins and other nutrients, adversely impacting both health and intelligence.

Mental health is another area. Microbiome-related research has shifted the diagnosis and treatment of mental disorders from primarily a cranial-based approach to whole-body neurology. Breakthroughs are occurring regularly and will likely accelerate. For example, research into autism by Italian molecular biologist Marco Ruggiero, M.D., Ph.D., has led to many of the discoveries regarding the existence and functioning of the human microbiome.[68]

With eight billion minds each having eight million genes to work with, the growth in knowledge about the complete human physiology's ecosystem should provide knowledge workers and enterprises with plenty of rewarding work for decades to come.

---

[68] James Jeffrey Bradstreet, Stefania Pacini and Marco Ruggiero, *A new methodology of viewing extra-axial fluid and cortical abnormalities in children with autism via transcranial ultrasonography*, Front. Hum. Neurosci., 15 January 2014.

Chapter 19

Core Values as Guideposts in a Turbulent World[69]

Succeeding in the global knowledge economy means leading, connecting, co-creating, and discovering at breakneck speed. Achieving and sustaining that level of performance demands staying focused on doing the right things, in the right way, at the right time, for the right reasons.

Today's market turbulence can instill a sense of panic, pressuring organizations to deviate from the principles upon which they were originally founded. You can see this in the many news stories and documentaries about thriving enterprises that have been ruined by lapses in ethics and morals, usually brought about by the temptation of shortcuts to easy riches.

---

[69] Adapted from Art Murray and Jeff Lesher, *Core Values Steady the Course in a Volatile World*, KMWorld Magazine, October, 2009.

Our tightly networked and transparent world has become very unforgiving. As we reinvent the enterprise, we need to bring core values front and center. We've already shown the importance of having a clear mission statement aligned with a concise set of goals and a well-planned strategy. In much the same way, every enterprise needs a clearly defined set of values-based criteria for making strategic and tactical decisions in a manner consistent with the legal, moral and ethical principles under which the organization operates.

Rather than getting into a long discussion on the definition of values, it would be better to list a few that we have found to be useful in providing clarity for navigating a complex and often confusing business climate.

<u>Core Value #1</u>: *Focus on creating, delivering, receiving and growing extraordinary value.*

If the frequent ups and downs in the financial markets have taught us anything, it should be that wealth isn't simply the amount of money you've managed to acquire. Rather, it's a measure of the value you create, the value you deliver, the value you receive and the value you keep and grow. Hopefully your definition of value extends beyond monetary value to include environmental, societal, and other impacts.

Tools such as value network analysis help quantify, visualize, and better enable the exchange of value. Use these and other tools to mine your social network—your brain trust—for intellectual assets that are hidden, overlooked, or underutilized. Keep in mind that whatever the value, the way in which it is created and delivered is just as important. No amount of money or personal satisfaction is worth crossing legal, moral or ethical boundaries.

<u>Top-level decision criterion</u>: Are you creating value in a way that's legal, moral and ethical?

<u>Core Value #2</u>: *Honor your commitments.*

Whether verbal or written, a contract is a contract. The old system of British common law remains the legal foundation for doing business in many countries as well as international law governing cross-border transactions. The basis for that legal system is simple: "*Do everything you've agreed to do.*" In a world of instant global communication, the response to not honoring a commitment may be swift and furious. In many ways, the social networking system can mete out punishment far more severe in terms of loss of reputation (which directly translates into loss of revenue) than any government judiciary.

<u>Top-level decision criterion</u>: Will you be able to deliver what you've promised (both explicitly and implicitly)?

<u>Core Value #3</u>: *Eat your own cooking.*

You might already be familiar with this expression. Actually doing it is another matter. People have little tolerance for someone saying one thing and doing another. If it's not good enough for you, why would anybody else want it?

<u>Top-level decision criterion</u>: Are you using what you're selling? Are you practicing what you're preaching?

<u>Core Value #4</u>: *Energy, focus and leverage are more important than time and money.*

This particular value has changed somewhat over the course of our journey to create the enterprise of the future. Its earliest incarnation was the familiar expression, "*time is money.*" We've even used, "*time is precious; treat it as such.*" But those didn't go far enough.

In the enterprise of the future, time is the great equalizer. It's evenly allocated regardless of one's location, age or place in society. And in a world of instant communication, it's the one resource you can't afford to waste. Once it's gone, it's gone forever. Whoever masters the discipline of setting and adhering to priorities will have a distinct advantage in the global marketplace. That means being able to carefully discriminate and pick the right things to do and the right way to do them, and delivering the desired result in the most efficient way possible.

<u>Top-level decision criterion</u>: Are you gaining the greatest leverage from your time, energy, and resources?

<u>Core Value #5</u>: *Always make a positive contribution to the evolution and growth of the individual, organization and society.*

We are well aware of the serious challenges and exciting opportunities we face as a society. Human potential is truly unlimited. Everything we do should move us closer to a better world, one in which we can continue to achieve new breakthroughs on a sustained basis. Stagnation, the status quo and "business as usual" are all unacceptable to anyone wanting to be a serious player in the global knowledge economy. As the size of our networked brain trust stretches into the billions, the world's body of knowledge will expand at an ever-accelerating pace. Every enterprise, from the single knowledge entrepreneur to the mega-conglomerate, should be making a positive contribution to the growth of the human race and the environment in which we live.

<u>Top-level decision criterion</u>: Are you consciously and methodically putting people in positions in which they can continually learn and grow, while keeping your enterprise learning and growing at the same time?

This list is by no means complete. You may certainly add to it. You are limited only by your imagination. Be bold, but brutally honest at the same time. In an unforgiving world, core values are the GPS of the 21st century enterprise.

Chapter 20

When It Comes To Trust, Less Is More[70]

Trust is a hot topic these days. In politics. National security. Food and drug safety. Business and finance. It's hard to find any area of life that doesn't rely on trust.

We've been grappling with the concept since the early days of envisioning the knowledge-sharing enterprise. For example, knowledge sharing, especially when learning from past mistakes, requires a great deal of trust. In a low-trust organization, people are afraid to share what they know. Knowledge flows are stifled.

One of the reasons trust is at an all-time low is because the trust footprint, which we defined in Chapter 6, Opportunity #3, is literally spread all over the place. It should come as no surprise that as an

---

[70] Adapted from Art Murray, *Building the High-Trust Enterprise*, KMWorld Magazine, May, 2017, and *All aboard the blockchain express*, KMWorld Magazine, April, 2015.

organization grows more powerful and less transparent, incidents of trust violations increase. We've seen this in complex offshore corporations, secretive intelligence agencies, large news networks and media outlets, and massive government bureaucracies.

Take, for example, the WikiLeaks *Vault 7* release exposing the CIA's "global covert hacking program." Its alleged weaponized malware arsenal can potentially affect millions of consumer electronic devices including smart phones, tablets, desktop computers and even some television sets.

As many as 5,000 people with security clearances are believed to have had knowledge of the program. This clearly presents a very large trust footprint, making it extremely difficult to identify the individuals or groups responsible for the leaks.

Regardless, the damage has already been done. Trust has been violated not only with regard to guarding a secret, but also regarding what was being done in secret.

In many instances, detecting and responding to trust violations happens too slowly. For example, the compromise of the U.S. Office of Personnel Management database containing the private records of millions of U.S. government employees and contractors holding security clearances is believed to have continued undetected for more than six months.

Given that backdrop, let's take a look at some of the ways you can create greater trust across your enterprise. One place to start is by reducing your trust footprint. It may sound counterintuitive, but when it comes to trust, *less is more*.

In the world of trusted systems, you'll find frequent use of the term trusted platform module (TPM), formerly referred to as the trusted computing base. TPM is defined by the Trusted Computing Group as: *"the set of functions and data that are common to all types of platform, which must be trustworthy if the subsystem is to be trustworthy; a logical definition in terms of protected capabilities and shielded locations."* [71]

Essentially, it boils down to this: the smaller the size or "footprint" of the TPM, the fewer the opportunities for compromise. That applies to both the human and technological aspects.

On the human side, we know that as organizations become very large, they often break down into smaller, isolated compartments that end up competing against each other. When that happens, the local missions of the various compartments ultimately take precedence over the broad, strategic mission of the enterprise. As a result, integrity and accountability are weakened. It actually becomes harder for the organization to hold onto its secrets.

To prevent that from happening, you should always be on guard against "mission creep" and the creation of localized, competing factions. As a leader, make sure your enterprise stays focused on the overall mission, along with the values that must be adhered to while achieving that mission.

On the technology side, there are many options. Here are just three of many potentially groundbreaking game-changers you need to watch closely and include in your future trust-building plans: *blockchain; homomorphic encryption; Double Helix.*

---

[71] Trusted Computing Group, *Protection Profile: PC Client Specific Trusted Platform Module,* TPM Family 1.2; Level 2 Revision 116 Version: 1.2, 2011.

Blockchain.

We've always envisioned the enterprise of the future as a massively interconnected virtual organization. One of the greatest challenges in making this vision a reality is finding a way to stitch all the pieces together in a meaningful, coordinated way.

This is particularly difficult for large global enterprises, smart cities and all levels of government. Forcing decision-making and control to the center slows everything down. Pushing it out to the edge speeds things up, but at the cost of increased fragmentation and redundancy.

In a traditional enterprise, the flow of goods, services and information has many interruptions. Timesheets, purchase orders and other ledger entries are validated internally by management as well as by outside auditing firms. Legal documents are witnessed and stamped by a notary. Employee backgrounds are investigated by a personnel security firm. Product quality is measured by a standards testing lab. All are separate, trusted entities and by nature involve slow and sometimes expensive processes.

Such approaches are also fraught with single points of failure of trust. Notable examples include cases ranging from Enron to Wells Fargo, from failed space launches to airline and cruise ship disasters. As the volume of data being processed continues to escalate, so does the risk.

At long last, a breakthrough may have finally arrived. It comes in the form of one of today's more disruptive innovations—a data structure known as a block chain. This simple yet elegant idea has the potential to change our entire notion of the enterprise, the economy and all of society.

A block chain is nothing more than a ledger maintained over a public peer-to-peer (P2P) network. The "secret sauce" isn't even secret. It's an open-source model.[72] This in itself greatly reduces the size of the TPM.

---

[72] Satoshi Nakamoto, *Bitcoin: A Peer-to-Peer Electronic Cash System.*

Ledger entries are digitally generated using a unique "hash" (a common indexing technique). A digital signature is added using the recipient's public encryption key and recorded in the block chain. Entries are validated using a clever puzzle-solving algorithm as a means of determining "proof of work." That makes it extremely difficult to compromise the system. It also minimizes the overall computational burden on the network, an important factor in P2P processing.

As a result, speed, volume, and accuracy are increased. The need for a trusted fiduciary such as a bank or accounting firm is eliminated. As such, the potential cost savings are substantial, especially considering the explosive growth in the number of items that will require tracking and monitoring.

Blockchain technology has the potential to dramatically transform how we interact with just about everyone and everything. Any document, person, organization, transaction, or object, from the smallest part to finished assembly, is fair game.

Many functions and activities would benefit: intellectual property protection; contractual obligations; marketing, sales and customer service (including tracking individual preferences); document authorship and authenticity; logistics and inventory management. The list goes on.

More importantly, enterprises can become better equipped to handle mass customization, where every product is unique not only in its physical configuration but also in how it interacts with the user. Add to that the ability to continually sense and respond to changes in the environment. Imagine custom pharmaceuticals uniquely formulated to each person's genetic makeup, metabolism and vital signs as measured by an internal array of body sensors. All while maintaining patient privacy.

Large companies like *IBM* and *Samsung* have major stakes in developing blockchain-based platforms and applications, including their *Autonomous Decentralized Peer-To-Peer Telemetry* (ADEPT) system, which was released in 2015.

You can see where all of this is going. Just-in-time is giving way to *just-ahead-of-time* (see Opportunity #4 in Chapter 6).

Old, trusted approaches will likely become overwhelmed and therefore less trustworthy. We have already seen this in the spate of data breaches making front-page news. Blockchain technology provides a way to address that vulnerability.

To be clear, challenges remain. Blockchain technology uses *public key infrastructure* (PKI) encryption, so it's reasonably secure from fraud, theft, corruption and the like. But anonymity is never 100 percent guaranteed.

Will the blockchain concept scale into the trillions? Will it hold up against cyberattacks? Will skeptical users embrace it, especially if it disrupts established professions, including finance, accounting, and law?

Will governments even allow it? Or will they demand some type of "back-door" access, possibly resulting in a skeptical public abandoning the idea altogether?

One thing is for certain: the current disintermediation trend will continue to whittle away at the "middle man," cutting out all those folks who take a percent here, a percent there, adding little if any value. Massive, slow-moving and expensive bureaucracies will find themselves becoming increasingly irrelevant. They may have worked well during the last century, but they have little hope of keeping up with the ongoing explosion in the volume of data.

Homomorphic encryption. Before encrypted data can be processed and analyzed, it must first be decrypted. When the analysis is completed, the results are re-encrypted for secure transmission and storage. The longer the data remains unencrypted, the more vulnerable it is to compromise. Homomorphic encryption solves that problem by allowing data to remain encrypted while it is being processed, including in the cloud. Although currently processing-intensive, it should become a viable technology within the next decade.

Double Helix. Funded by DARPA and currently under development at the University of Virginia and the University of New Mexico, *Double Helix* is an autonomous reasoning system that increases assurance not necessarily by reducing the trust footprint, but by making the TPM a moving target. It does that by rapidly altering the protected system's binary code, keeping any attackers continuously off guard. While autonomous reasoning systems can actually increase the size of the TPM, they more than make up for it in speed of threat detection and response. Still in the early R&D stage, it's worth paying close attention to this and similar efforts underway at DARPA.

Actions to take

Creating a high-trust enterprise requires that well-known triad of people, processes and technology, with the ultimate goal of eliminating any and all opportunities for violating trust. This means doing everything you can to minimize the trust footprint, which in turn means leaving nothing to chance. The best way to do that is through increased transparency.

That doesn't mean compromising sensitive information. Rather, it entails exposing performance by consistently maintaining open and honest accountability.

Another step you can take is monitoring the public discourse on social media. Growing numbers of people are on some form of social media (now numbering in the billions). This represents an extremely valuable information source you can't ignore. It can help you discover clues of possible trust erosion ahead of time and take corrective action before it's too late.

Finally, be clear about your mission and values (Chapter 19). Most of all, be congruent. Nothing builds trust more than saying what you mean, and doing what you said you would do. Trust and accountability go hand in hand, and along with them, more ethical decision-making and a reputation for a high degree of integrity.

Chapter 21

Case Example: Stitching the Pieces Together[73]

Building the enterprise of the future means stretching organizational boundaries far beyond their traditional limits. Some of those boundaries may end up disappearing altogether.

A key dynamic is the tension between small businesses and large, legacy institutions. The knowledge enterprise, or *knowledge web*, as we'll call it, aims to link these two very different types of organizations together in a synergistic way. The small gives the large greater agility. The large gives the small greater leverage. Ideally, it should be a win-win proposition.

---

[73] Adapted from Dr. Arthur Murray and Michael Runde, *Science and Technology Parks and Areas of Innovation as Knowledge Hubs: Balancing Innovation and Business Development*, 31st World Conference on Science Parks and Areas of Innovation, Doha, Qatar, 20 October, 2014.

Let's take a look at one such a knowledge web, in which a group of pioneering world trade centers, science parks, the Consumer Electronics Show, and numerous other organizations are slowly discovering that the whole is indeed much greater than the sum of the parts. But first, we need to take a look at the typical startup company and how knowledge flows begin to get bogged down as the company transitions through its various growth phases.

The startup stage

By their very nature, startup companies are small enough that knowledge flows within their brain trust–usually the founders and a few close advisors–are rarely a problem (see Figure 21-1). It also helps that the critical knowledge to be shared is limited to a few key topics such as experimental design, meeting development milestones, and obtaining early buy-in from customers and investors.

The knowledge infrastructure in this case often consists of a conference table and white board. Decisions, a key output of any knowledge exchange, are frequent and typically made on-the-spot.

For example, the sales rock star gets a question from a potential client about a need that would require putting together a customized solution. The scientist likes the idea. The lead developer balks at the change in requirements, while the money person demands up-front payment with premium pricing, which elicits a stern grimace from the sales rock star. After going around the table a number of times, an agreement is reached.

The impact of scaling on knowledge flows

Now consider what happens years later, as the company breaks through the 20 million-dollar sales barrier and reaches the 100-employee mark. The organization will in all likelihood resemble the chart in Figure 21-2.

"The Scientist"
One of only a few
who understand
the theory behind
the technology

"The Money Person"
Good with numbers;
understands and closely
controls cash flow

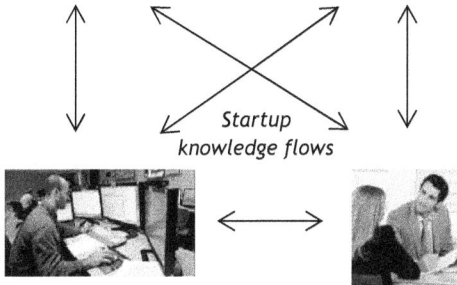

Startup
knowledge flows

"The Techie"
Lead developer;
understands what is and
what is not "doable"

"The Sales Rock Star"
Networker; relationship-builder;
understands the competitive
environment and pricing from
the buyer's perspective

Figure 21-1. The startup company is naturally organized to share knowledge

The same type of sales opportunity pops up, this time from a large company halfway around the world. The scope, scale, and complexity are one-to-two orders of magnitude greater than the opportunities in the startup phase. In addition, the new opportunity requires taking on additional suppliers, financing, and all the risks associated with international sales.

The office where the opportunity originated is now many miles and organizational layers from the nascent outbound logistics office. No longer taking place around a conference table, the decision process has slowed considerably.

Figure 21-2. Knowledge flows break into silos as startup companies enter the growth phase

Legal counsel needs extra time to grapple with complex tax regimes and customs regulations. Finance attempts to put systems in place to handle foreign currency transactions and international banking. Outbound logistics and training need time to ramp up in order to support the language and culture of the new customer base.

A real example of what can happen when organizations become very large and their knowledge gets trapped in silos recently occurred in a new $100M emergency treatment facility which was added to a hospital in a small U.S. city. In the new, ultra-modern wing, ER doctors were experiencing difficulty using their stethoscopes. Air ducts, strategically placed to maximize air flows, were directly above the patient beds. But the noise from the diffusers impeded the physicians' ability to hear the subtle sounds needed to quickly assess a patient's condition.[74]

---

[74] Art Murray, *Smart hospitals: Transformational medicine for the knowledge age, Part 1*, KMWorld Magazine, July/August 2012.

This was clearly a case of a clogged knowledge pipeline. Two obvious dots that should have been connected were not. In designing and building a new emergency healthcare center, neither the architects nor the HVAC (heating, ventilation and air conditioning) engineers fully took into account the needs of the people who mattered the most, the end users: the doctors, nurses and patients who would actually be using the facility.

Let's take a look at another real-world example of knowledge flows, this time involving a World Trade Center and a small business.

A knowledge-sharing success story

Signature Worldwide is a U.S.-based training company located in Dublin, Ohio's tech corridor, directly adjacent to the city's Entrepreneurial Center and Technology Park. Founded in 1986, Signature originally served the hospitality industry. In 2002, looking to expand into the global marketplace, the company approached the World Trade Center (WTC) Dulles Airport for help.

A World Trade Centers Association (WTCA) licensee since 1997, WTC Dulles has access to a vast network of over 15,000 WTC tenant companies worldwide. This is in addition to its own network of clients and partners, many of which are located in Dulles Airport's backyard in Loudoun County, Virginia, which has come to be known as the Washington DC *Netplex*. It got this name based on the fact that over half of all U.S. internet traffic passes through the county's massive underground fiber optic network and highly secure data centers every day. The region also boasts more technology professionals than anywhere else in the nation. This gives WTC Dulles unique positioning to offer services beyond those of traditional WTCs.

It would be overwhelming for Signature's sales staff to comb through all 15,000 WTCA tenant companies to find the right matches. That's where WTC Dulles' extensive knowledge web fits in (see Figure 21-3).

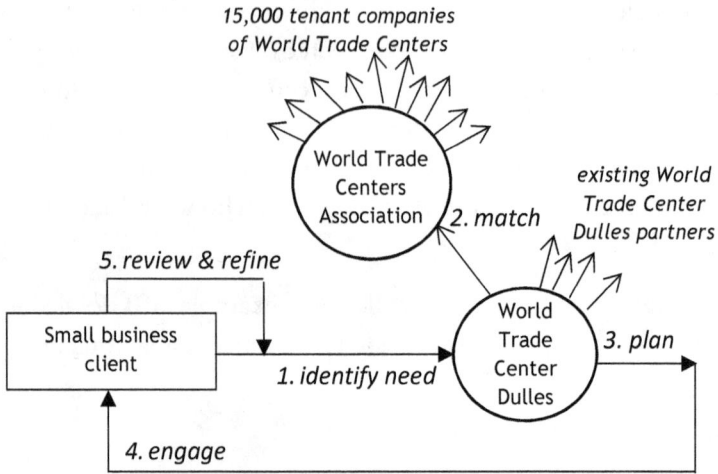

Figure 21-3. Initial Knowledge Web

By applying their understanding of Signature's goals and objectives (step 1), along with their know-how and expert insights into the vast WTCA network, WTC Dulles staff proceeded to refine the list of candidate customers and partners to a more manageable set (step 2).

Several selection criteria were taken into account. Among the many candidate companies identified, those known to have an entrepreneurial mindset and friendly inclination toward early-stage companies were chosen. The choice of business model was another important consideration. The list of candidates was further refined to include those with CEOs known to favor licensing as opposed to franchising.

Finally, the all-important ingredient of culture was added. For this aspect, if it was determined that an American style of training would fit within the candidate customer's culture, while at the same time provide new insights that could help grow the host nation's hospitality sector, that candidate rose to the top of the list.

This knowledge-based filtering process resulted in narrowing down the list of candidate companies to less than 100. After making the appropriate introductions, meetings were set up (step 3), and the client entered into discussions with each candidate customer/business partner (step 4). Based on feedback obtained during the various encounters, the list was further refined (step 5).

In the months and years which followed, with the help of WTC Dulles, Signature's market expanded from the USA to forty other countries. Today, Signature Worldwide serves 90 countries from its US headquarters, with regional offices in Cyprus, Argentina, Brazil, Canada and Thailand.

Building and growing a global knowledge web

It was at this point that WTC Dulles realized it needed to scale its services. They did this by a combination of process innovation and technology.

Figure 21-4 illustrates the knowledge sharing platform being developed by WTC Dulles. It consists of three layers: a network layer, a data layer, and an application layer.

A global knowledge enterprise must allow easy data accessibility for knowledge sharing and collaboration while protecting proprietary information. For this, WTC Dulles discovered that one of its local partners was in the process of testing a prototype platform for secure collaboration and data-sharing over an open, unclassified network such as the internet. They plan to incorporate this technology into the initial network layer.

With a secure network as a foundation, services offered by the next-generation science park and world trade center will include access to a rapidly expanding database of technology providers and other businesses (the data layer). In addition to the 15,000 World Trade Center tenants we mentioned earlier, the extended knowledge web also includes 128,000 companies who are tenants in science parks belonging to the International Association of Science Parks and Areas of Innovation (IASP). WTC Dulles is currently the only World Trade Center that is also a member of IASP.

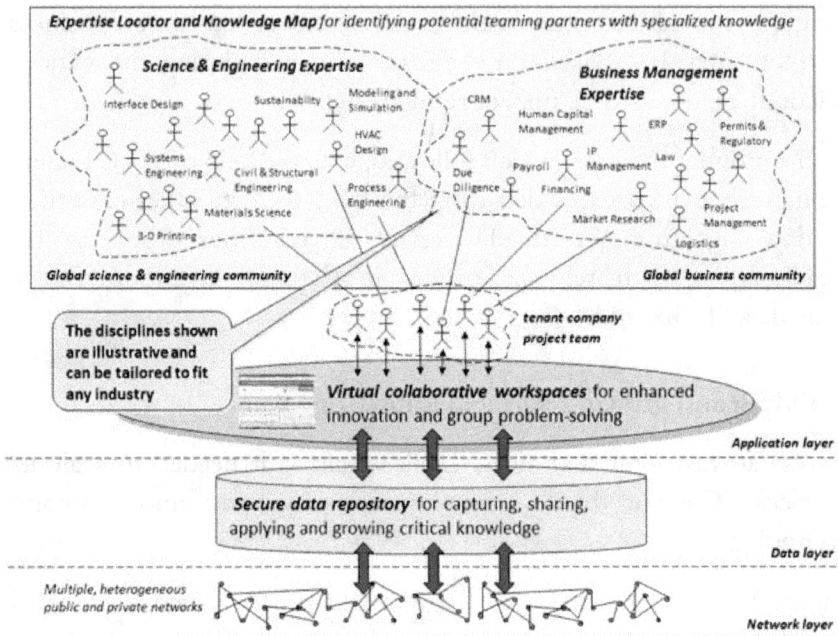

Figure 21-4. Knowledge-sharing platform

The top, or application layer, is the "sweet spot" for knowledge sharing and collaboration. Two relevant applications are *knowledge maps* and *expertise locator* systems. Just as a GPS app finds and directs users to a physical location, knowledge maps and expertise locators help users locate a source for the knowledge they are seeking. Such tools have proven extremely useful for pairing businesses with suppliers and partners providing technology and other services.

Once a credible knowledge source is identified and vetted, knowledge transfer/exchange is enabled through a virtual collaborative workspace. Over time, the knowledge grows and improves. Systems for building and maintaining lessons-learned and best practices repositories (documenting what works, what doesn't work, and why, based on previous experience), along with communities of practice (CoP) platforms are common tools for this purpose.

WTC Dulles' rapidly growing knowledge web is shown in Figure 21-5. In addition to their access to World Trade Center and science park tenant companies, WTC Dulles has entered into direct partnership agreements with trade centers in Italy, India, China, Uruguay and the U.S., as well as an economic free zone (Daegu) and Area of Innovation (Daedeok), both in South Korea.

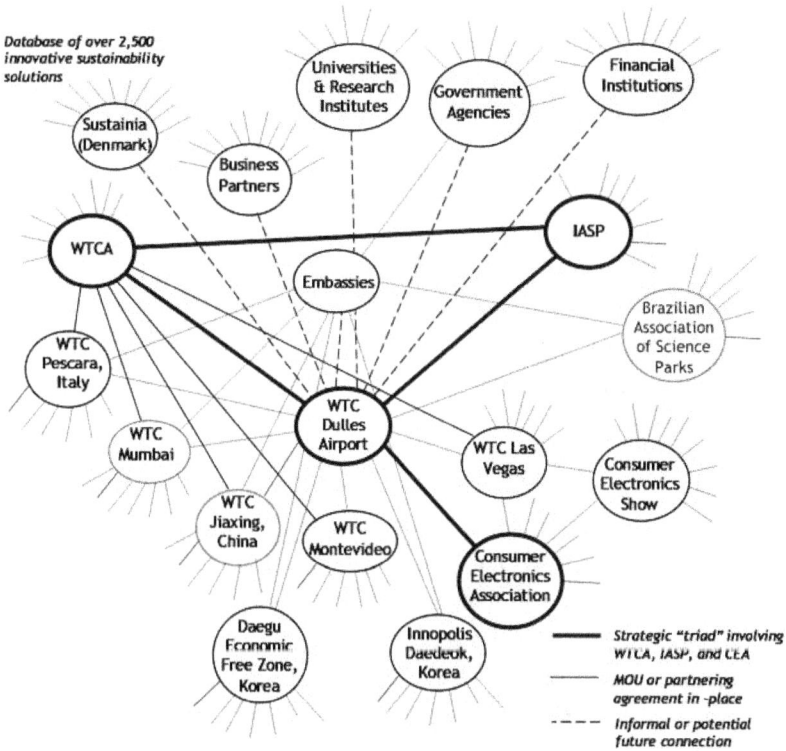

Figure 21-5. World Trade Center Dulles' global knowledge web

WTC Dulles has also entered into a strategic partnership with the Consumer Electronics Association (CEA), organizer of one of the world's largest trade shows, the Consumer Electronics Show (CES) held every January in Las Vegas. One of WTC Dulles' contributions to this alliance has been collaborating with the WTC Las Vegas and CES on the new Eureka Park segment of the show, which after only four years of operation has grown from 28 exhibitors to over 200. The addition of CAE completes a strategic "triad" consisting of science parks (including areas of innovation or "clusters"), world trade centers, and a major trade association, linking innovators, businesses and consumers.

WTC Dulles' close proximity to Washington DC and its collective experience in government contracting make it an ideal partner for science park and world trade center tenant companies seeking to do business with U.S. federal, state and local governments. Relationships with local universities, research institutes and commercial businesses, when combined with this extensive government reach, form a body of knowledge aimed at providing small- to medium-sized companies outside the U.S. with a "soft landing" capability. Relationships with regional organizations such as the Brazilian Association of Science Parks add to the opportunities. Direct access to embassies and their trade desks further expands the knowledge web, as do the many relationships with financial institutions specializing in global markets.

Countless other organizations could potentially be included. *Sustainia*, for example, is a Copenhagen-based "innovation tank" that has spent the last few years building a database of best practices in sustainability, including many "grass roots" projects in frontier nations that have the potential for being adapted and migrated to other locales. Each year, Sustainia recognizes the top 100 innovations spanning ten different sustainability categories. The publicity helps raise awareness and connect innovators to funding sources to scale up and commercialize their ideas. Their database currently stands at over 2,500 solutions and is rapidly growing.

The dashed lines in Figure 21-5 show the knowledge flows that would result from these added relationships. Whether or not a world trade center or science park tenant succeeds in forming partners and responding to an opportunity, the lessons-learned from that engagement can be captured, adapted, and re-applied to other, noncompeting companies in the same country or region.

What it all means

As a result of this new "knowledge web" way of thinking, world trade centers and science parks are waking up to the realization that renting office space and shared receptionist and janitorial services are outdated business models. In today's market such resources, although essential, are useless without the ability of tenant companies to access, share, and apply knowledge. The good news is, with AI and cloud-based platforms, access to knowledge resources can be "rented" out in much the same way.

The result will be faster product-to-market cycles, enabled by the ability to quickly learn and make adjustments from both successes and failures, a key factor in successful innovation. Overall, less time and resources will be wasted by repeated errors, duplicated effort, slow technology transfer pipelines, and other problems impacting the smooth transfer of knowledge.

Just like WTC Dulles, you can build your enterprise knowledge web in much the same way.

Chapter 22

Final Thoughts (at least for now)

Our final thought for this book is that there are no final thoughts. The leading, connecting, co-creating and discovering never ends. The enterprise of the future that we envision today will not be the same as the enterprise of the future we will envision and build tomorrow.

If you're having trouble wrapping your head around that non-final, final thought, great. That's the mindset you'll need to succeed in an increasingly complex, fast-changing world. You'll also need to decide whether you want to be leading the changes, riding the wave, or falling hopelessly behind.

Building a Permanent Body of Knowledge of the Human Race

Billions of interconnected minds have the potential for generating a body of knowledge of unimagined proportion. The challenges and opportunities we discussed in Part III are very real and need to be addressed. We can't just "hope and pray" that all will turn out well. As stewards of the planet we must pool our intellectual resources. This in turn mandates the open co-creation and sharing of knowledge.

Past history has shown a marked tendency for repeating mistakes. As the world becomes more complex and fast-changing, it also becomes much less forgiving. Mistakes made today could prove extremely costly downstream.

We need to develop a world-wide resource for capturing, sharing, applying and growing knowledge on a large scale. This can be viewed as a 21st-century version of the Great Library at Alexandria, or a virtual "Beit al-Hikma." It will need to be globally distributed and robust, rather than concentrated in one location.

Through a knowledge resource of this magnitude, we can become much better at avoiding repeated mistakes and quickly correcting the errors we make. It will allow us to make the best use of our precious resources and build a truly sustainable global knowledge economy that will bring prosperity for ages to come.

The message is clear: if we have the power to produce nanorobots, manipulate DNA and stem cells, and extract and burn every last molecule of fossil fuel from the earth, we need to understand that many of the resulting event chains will likely be irreversible. We are going to need every tool and brain at our disposal, including a few new ones.

Turning risk into opportunity

Advances in technology can be both constructive and destructive. So be sure to use them to your advantage. For example, you can use an assortment of tools such as big data analytics, value network analysis, and semantic analysis to discover hidden trends and patterns that can help you better prepare for and respond to emerging threats as well as opportunities, both internal and external. Remember, you can be the one disrupting your industry, rather than reacting to somebody else's disruption. Finally, make sure that access to your critical data, as well as your key subject matter experts and decision makers, doesn't have to pass through a single choke point.

Ride the wave. And keep on riding it, for as long as it lasts. History is replete with technology-driven "singularities" which moved us kicking and screaming from hunter-gatherers to farmers to assembly line workers to information workers to knowledge workers.

The current wave still has a long way to go. There's plenty of thinking, innovating and discovery that needs to be done. So you might as well hop on board. Use machines as your tools, not as your master. But remember to keep humans "in-the-loop," especially when making critical decisions. The temptation to cede decisions to machines (for example, high-frequency trading in the financial markets) can be strong.

Be selective. Let machines control your refrigerator and lighting systems. Even your automobiles. But don't let them control your thinking. Otherwise, you might as well go ahead and implant that computer chip into your skull now, and dive into the *Matrix*.

Remain vigilant. Armed with the right knowledge, you'll be able to continue blazing a trail to a brighter future, no matter what happens along the way.

Good luck, and be sure to periodically visit *enterpriseofthefuture.org* from time-to-time. We'll continue refining the framework, showcasing organizations who are transforming themselves and how they're doing it, and answering your questions as best we can.

And remember: *"We co-create the future by what we do today."* Or better yet: *"We co-create the future by what we do right now."*

You know, *"just ahead of time…"*

Appendix A: Enterprise of the Future Framework

Leading: Co-creating new business ecosystems

<u>Key roles</u>: Chairman; CEO; Director.

<u>Ownership of</u>: Vision; mission; goals; strategy; governance.

Guiding Principles	Key Focus Areas	Attributes
Enlightened business decisions Strategic alignment throughout the enterprise	Cultural embodiment of core values	Legal, moral and ethical principles under which the organization operates are known and form the basis for decisions made at every level
	Anticipatory business intelligence	Data-driven analytics are augmented with biological/social/behavior-driven models
	Enlightened business decisions	Business decisions consistently take financial, ethical, societal and environmental stewardship into account
	Adaptive strategy formulation	The process for formulating, planning and executing strategy is understood and practiced Theory of change is a key part of strategic forecasting and strategy formulation
	Agile execution	Master strategy and sub-strategies are clear to everyone and are refined as conditions change Everything the organization does is aligned with strategy Performance is measured and tracked Innovation and learning occur simultaneously

Connecting: Evolving, adaptive infrastructure nexus

<u>Key roles</u>: CIO; CTO; Security Director; Facilities Director.

<u>Ownership of</u>: Enterprise Architecture; external interfaces; information assurance; all aspects of security.

Guiding Principles	Key Focus Areas	Attributes
Technology is considered an enabler, rather than an end unto itself	Self-aware, resilient value networks (knowing who knows what, how, and why)	The network "sees itself," knows who knows what, and the value each person brings to the table Social/Value Network Analysis is practiced and applied Self-organization is encouraged and supported People actively participate in global knowledge-sharing communities; organizational boundaries are minimized Techniques for successful virtual collaboration are practiced and refined The right expertise can be easily tapped when needed The organization not only knows what it knows, but also "grows what it knows" Open communication and the free flow of knowledge across the enterprise are encouraged and enabled The capacity for identifying, resisting, absorbing and restoring business operations following a major adverse event is maintained and continuously upgraded
	Evolving Knowledge Enterprise Architecture	An Enterprise Architecture which aligns technology with business processes, performance drivers, and strategy, is established and maintained

Guiding Principles	Key Focus Areas	Attributes
		Formal tool selection processes are in-place and coordinated
		Technology infrastructure provides ease of access while maximizing privacy and security
	Total systems integration	Key components across the enterprise are woven together into a "self-aware" system of systems
		Balance exists between localization and centralization; local systems are seamlessly connected into an integrated whole.

Co-creating and delivering extraordinary value: Agile, intelligent systems and processes

<u>Key roles</u>: COO; CMO; CFO

<u>Ownership of</u>: Business models, systems and processes; KPIs (key performance indicators).

Guiding Principles	Key Focus Areas	Attributes
Effective, efficient and pervasive collaboration	Value co-creation/exchange	The value of tangible and intangible assets is known and tracked; Value gaps and opportunities are quickly identified and quantified
	Business Model Innovation	All aspects of the business model are measured and evaluated on a regular basis New means for exchanging value are developed and tested on a regular basis
	Streamlined, embedded decision processes	Innovation and learning occur more by design than by chance The knowledge life cycle is an integral part of all work and decision processes The entire workforce understands, expects, promotes and manages change
	Key performance drivers known and measured	Industry clockspeed is known and compared to internal development cycles Underlying core capabilities needed to achieve the desired level of performance are understood and managed

Making breakthrough discoveries: Growth- and fulfillment-oriented work environments

Key roles: CKO, CLO, VP R&D.

Ownership of: Intellectual asset portfolio; innovation-and-learning growth cycle.

Guiding Principles	Key Focus Areas	Attributes
Creating the best environment for leading a balanced, fulfilled life	Life-supporting and fulfilling work	People are passionate about their work, and are driven by a greater goal
		Attracting, retaining, and growing talent are given high priority; compensation systems are performance-based, and take risk vs. reward into account
	Engaged workforce	Lessons-learned and best-practice improvements are habitually sought before, during and after a major task or activity
	Personal and organizational growth	Each individual knows his/her strengths/weaknesses and has a personal development plan
		Personal knowledge contributes to organizational knowledge and vice versa
	Systems-thinking mindset	People see the total picture
		Differing perspectives and viewpoints are always taken into account
		Deep learning methods are understood and habitually practiced

Appendix B: Additional Resources

This book provides only a glimpse into the rapidly expanding body of knowledge about building and growing a fast-learning enterprise of the future.

Here are just a few of the related topics, along with a small sampling of additional references, should you want to explore further. Please note that these references are in addition to the footnotes provided in the main body of the book.

For updates on the enterprise of the future, visit:

enterpriseofthefuture.org

and visit our companion sites at:

adaptivedeeplearning.com

lessonslearnedworld.com

Leadership

John Addison, *Real Leadership: 9 Simple Practices for Leading and Living with Purpose*, McGraw-Hill Education, 2016.

Strategic Forecasting

techchast.org delivers an organized and visually well-presented resource for tracking world-changing future technologies, using a unique blend of continuous Delphi and other techniques.

Strategy

W. Chan Kim and Renee Mauborgne, *Blue Ocean Strategy: How To Create Uncontested Market Space and Make the Competition Irrelevant*, Harvard Business School Press, 2005.

Rich Horwath, *Deep Dive: The Proven Method for Building Strategy, Focusing Your Resources, and Taking Smart Action*, Greenleaf Book Group, 2011.

Performance measurement

Douglas W. Hubbard, *How To Measure Anything: Finding the Value of "Intangibles" in Business*, 2nd ed., Wiley, 2010.

Co-creating

Tony Schwartz, *The Way We're Working Isn't Working: The Four Forgotten Needs That Energize Great Performance*, Free Press, 2010.

Scott Hartley, *The Fuzzie and the Techie: Why the Liberal Arts Will Rule the Digital World*, Houghton Mifflin Harcourt, 2017.

Discovering

John Lewis, *The Explanation Age* (3rd edition), 2013. This resource will guide you through the various phases of discovery, ranging from disrupting the status quo to ideation, design, and implementing change. You'll find an impressive collection of templates and examples, plus a model Lewis calls the *innate lesson cycle*. He also provides ways to capture and express for future reference the thinking behind an idea, including options that were considered along the way, which is rarely done in practice.

Michael Nielson, *Reinventing Discovery: The New Era of Networked Science*, Princeton University Press, 2012.

Alex Bennet, David Bennet, Joyce Avedisian, *The Course of Knowledge: A 21st Century Theory*, MQIPress, 2015.

David Bennet, Alex Bennet, Robert Turner, *Expanding the Self: the Intelligent Complex Adaptive Learning System, a New Theory of Adult Learning*, MQIPress, 2015.

Bernie Trilling and Charles Fadel, *21st Century Skills: Learning for Life in Our Times*, Jossey-Bass, 2009.

Michael J. Gelb, *How to Think Like Leonardo da Vinci: Seven Steps to Genius Every Day*, Dell, 2000.

Learning environments

Leon van Schaik, *Spatial Intelligence: New Futures for Architecture*, John Wiley & Sons, Ltd., 2008.

David Thornburg, *From the Campfire to the Holodeck: Creating Engaging and Powerful 21st Century Learning Environments*, Jossey-Bass, 2014.

We're also influenced by the work of our colleague Dr. Dan Holtshouse, whose Workplace of the Future framework looks at four types of environments for living, working and learning: 1) physical space; 2) information space; 3) organizational space; 4) cognitive space.

See kmworld.com/Articles/Column/The-Future-of-the-Future/The-Future-of-the-Future-The-future-workplace-15811.aspx

also:

Knowledge Work 2020: Thinking Ahead About Knowledge Work, On the Horizon, Vol 18, Number 3, 2010.

The Global Knowledge Economy

Robert Guest, *Borderless Economics: Chinese Sea Turtles, Indian Fridges and the New Fruits of Global Capitalism*, Palgrave Macmillan, 2011.

George Gilder, *Knowledge and Power: The Information Theory of Capitalism and How It Is Revolutionizing Our World*, Regnery, 2013.

Risk and resilience

David Apgar, *Risk Intelligence: Learning to Manage What We Don't Know*, Harvard Business School Press, 2006.

Nassim Nicholas Taleb, *Antifragile: Things That Gain from Disorder*, Random House, 2012.

William R. Forstchen, *One Second After*, Forge, 2009.

Karl E. Weick and Kathleen M. Sutcliffe, *Managing the Unexpected: Resilient Performance in an Age of Uncertainty*, 2nd ed., Jossey-Bass, 2007.

Smart Cities and Social Cohesion

Richard Florida, *The New Urban Crisis: How Our Cities Are Increasing Inequality, Deepening Segregation, and Failing the Middle Class – And What We Can Do About It*, Basic Books, 2017.

Triple bottom line/sustainability/basic human needs

Daniel Christian Wahl, *Designing Regenerative Cultures*, Creative Commons, Triarchy Press, 2016.

Howard G. Buffett, *Forty Chances: Finding Hope In a Hungry World*, Simon & Schuster, 2013.

Acknowledgements

This book would not have been possible without the knowledge, wisdom and insights of an amazing and diverse group of people who at various times came together to help lead, connect, co-create and discover something called the enterprise of the future. Special thanks go out to…

Professor Michael Stankosky, co-founder of the George Washington University Institute for Knowledge and Innovation (GWU/IKI), currently the International Institute for Knowledge and Innovation (I2KI), who first came up with the idea for the Enterprise of the Future and led the development of a groundbreaking academic program in Knowledge and Innovation Management, with hundreds of masters and doctoral-level graduates, along with a research framework so we could quickly move various aspects of that idea out into practice.

Kent Greenes, KM thought leader and the first Chief Knowledge Officer for two large, international companies and co-founder of the Enterprise of the Future program at GWU/IKI.

William Halal, GWU Professor Emeritus, co-founder of GWU/IKI and founder of TechCast Global, LLC, which provides unique insights into future trends and their impact on business and society as a whole.

Francesco Calabrese, Managing Director of I2KI, whose doctoral and post-doctoral research into the four pillars of KM formed the basis for our enterprise of the future framework, and whose company, Enterprise Excellence Management Group, Inc., provided numerous opportunities to put that framework into practice, and **Joanne Freeman** and **Katharine Dill**, who worked tirelessly on organizing, coordinating and orchestrating our many gatherings in various locations throughout the Washington, DC area.

Professor Barry Silverman, University of Pennsylvania, who, as founder of GWU's Institute for Artificial Intelligence, planted the seeds of knowledge engineering which eventually grew into the broader discipline of KM.

Timothy Tong, former Dean of GWU's School of Engineering and Applied Science and now President of Hong Kong Polytechnic University, for handing us the keys to the Home of the Future Lab at the GWU Virginia Science & Technology campus and enabling us to springboard it into the Enterprise of the Future Lab.

Hugh McKellar, now retired editor-in-chief of KMWorld and current editor Sandra Haimila for supporting us with the publication of over 75 articles in the series: *The Future of the Future*; and Hugh, along with **Jane Dysart**, co-chairs of the annual KMWorld Conference, for promoting and participating in our many workshops and sessions over the past 15 years.

Dan Holtshouse, former Director, Corporate Strategy for Xerox and past Executive-In-Residence at GWU/IKI, for his tireless explorations into improving the workplace and building the workforce of the future.

French Caldwell, Gartner Fellow, for his participation in our many forums and for his sponsorship in making Gartner's massive body of research available to our team.

Mirghani Mohamed, for negotiating agreements with a variety of platform vendors and for keeping our testbed infrastructure at the Enterprise of the Future Lab up and running.

Professor Kamen Lozev, South-West University 'Neofit Rilski' – Blagoevgrad, Bulgaria, our past visiting Fulbright scholar, who keeps us grounded in the philosophical aspects of the knowledge sciences, as well as applying our framework in the areas of military and defense diplomacy.

Professor Vincent Ribière, Bangkok University, who expanded our efforts into the EU, the ASEAN region, and beyond.

Rudy Garrity, Founder of the American Learnership Forum, for leading the way to a mindful way of being as central to building a productive, fulfilled, and growth-oriented workforce aimed at leaving the world a better place than when we entered it.

Alex and David Bennet, co-founders of the Mountain Quest Institute, who along with **Bo Newman** (KM Forum), **Tom McCabe** (Expanded Consciousness Institute), John Lewis (Explanation Age, LLC), and Franc Calabrese conducted a knowledge sciences retreat in December, 2012, helping to reveal that knowledge also has deep, inner, subjective components that are all too often overlooked.

Paul Prueitt, Applied Knowledge Sciences, Inc. and founder of the Second School, and **Tom Adi** (ReadWare) for pushing the boundaries of knowledge transfer into the realms of applied semiotics, deep learning and deep semantics, and taking a lot of arrows in the process, as do many pioneers.

Paul Wormeli, founder and Director Emeritus of the Institute for Justice Information Systems (IJIS), for his tireless efforts at promoting and enabling knowledge sharing across multiple, diverse organizations by adopting standards and through changes in policy and practices.

Michael Runde, President, World Trade Center Dulles Airport, for his tireless efforts to build the World Trade Center and Science Park of the Future, and **Lowell B. Weiner, D.D.S.**, for doing the same in the fields of integrative dentistry and medicine.

Mark Minevich, a.k.a. "Global Mark" (Council on Competitiveness), and **Joseph Okpaku, Sr.**, CEO of Telecom Africa, who got us thinking about the future way back when we were only at six billion minds, just a little more than a decade ago.

John Alden, former senior research fellow at Accenture's Institute for Strategic Change, who along with **Andreas Andreou**, Research and Innovation Strategist at Gensler, gave us the original inspiration for the strategy pyramid which forms the cornerstone of much of our field practice.

Laszlo Horvath, founder and CEO of ActiveMedia and a frequent participant in our forums.

Ed Helvey, founder of "Live Freely," and his fellow "professional nomads," for providing living proof that you can co-create, deliver, receive and grow value from any place, at any time.

RADM Roger Gilbertson (USN-ret.), for always offering a fresh look at how to view knowledge.

David Martin, founder of M-CAM International and creator of the Global Innovation Commons, for never failing to come up with new insights into creating and exchanging value in all its many forms.

Richard Van West Charles, M.D. (Guyana Water Incorporated); **Dan Costantini** (L3); **Andrea Walsh** (Willis Towers Watson); **Charlie Ratliff, Sherrie Stein, Sean O'Connor** and the KM Team at Aera Energy; for bravely sticking their necks out and allowing us to test the theories and apply and refine our tools, methods, and practices in their organizations.

Our colleagues at Applied Knowledge Sciences, Inc., including **Ken Wheaton**, for keeping us visually-oriented, and along with **Bill Linn** and **Tom Beckman**, for putting many parts of the enterprise of the future framework into practice while withstanding multiple barrages of attacks with arrows, swords, and other sharp objects.

Annie Greene, **Gabrielle McLaughlin**, and the many doctoral researchers and faculty in the KM program in the School of Engineering and Applied Science at GWU.

Jeff Lesher, Akash Shukla, Azamat Abdoullaev, Greg Larsen, Nola Joyce, Sharon Hull, M.D., and many others already mentioned above, for their contributions to our KMWorld series: *The Future of the Future*.

Hassan Syed (Bir Ventures) and **Charles Chow** (East-West Group, Singapore) and many of those already named above, for their careful and insightful review of this book's draft manuscript.

ACKNOWLEDGEMENTS

Our many corporate sponsors, including UTI, L3, the Pan American Health Organization, The US Air Force SBIR Program, and Lockheed Martin.

Index

About the author

For over thirty years, Dr. Art Murray and his teams have helped individuals and organizations capture, share, and grow their deeply embedded knowledge. Clients include government agencies, non-profit organizations, and companies of all sizes across the globe.

He is CEO of Applied Knowledge Sciences, Inc., and Chief Technology Officer of the Second School Network. He holds a B.S.E.E. from Lehigh University, and the M.E.A. and D.Sc. degrees from The George Washington University. He is the author of the book *Deep Learning Manual: The knowledge explorer's guide to self-discovery in education, work, and life.* His column *The Future of the Future* has appeared in KMWorld Magazine for the past eleven years.

www.ingramcontent.com/pod-product-compliance
Lightning Source LLC
Chambersburg PA
CBHW060014210326
41520CB00009B/885